THE WEST IN CRISIS

BY JAMES P. WARBURG

The West in Crisis

JAMES P. WARBURG

DOUBLEDAY & COMPANY, INC., GARDEN CITY, NEW YORK

1959

This book is dedicated to the memory of a great and good citizen of the United States and of the world,

MARSHALL FIELD III

and to the following friends and fellow workers for peace, none of whom is responsible for anything in these pages but from each of whom I have received valuable help, encouragement, or inspiration:

Max Ascoli	John K. Galbraith
Joseph Barnes	Arthur H. Holcombe
Lord Boyd-Orr	Walter Lippmann
Henry B. Cabot	Avrahm Mezerik
Grenville Clark	Clarence Pickett
Norman Cousins	Sir John Slessor
Vera M. Dean	Norman Thomas

I am also deeply grateful to my wife, Joan, and to my sister, Bettina Grimson, for many helpful suggestions; to Ruth G. van den Bogaert for the preparation of the manuscript; and to Louis Siegel for correcting the proofs.

JAMES P. WARBURG

We can't sit about, waiting for some felicitous accident of history that may somehow make the world all right. Time is running against us. . . .

GENERAL OMAR N. BRADLEY

PREFACE

This book has been prompted not only by deep concern but by a feeling close to despair—despair on the part of one who is enough of an optimist to believe that man was not put upon this earth merely in order to destroy himself; and that *homo sapiens,* despite his inherent weaknesses, is endowed with moral sensibility and the capacity for rational thought and action.

Such a belief is not easy to reconcile with contemporary human behavior, especially with the behavior of that privileged portion of the human race which has for centuries enjoyed the maximum of freedom and opportunity.

One might conceivably be sufficiently objective to view the possible end of Western civilization with equanimity, realizing that throughout past millennia the decline and fall of one segment of the human race has been succeeded by the rise and efflorescence of another. Such aloof objectivity would be not only unnatural but unwarranted. The world has become too small and man has become too wise in unwisdom for the historical pattern to continue. The crisis of Western civilization has become the crisis of humanity—the crisis not only of the guilty few but of the innocent masses of mankind.

It may seem presumptuous for a mere individual to attempt to contribute toward stemming the world's headlong rush to destruction. The author makes no apology. Only the aggregate of individual efforts offers any hope, no matter how feeble any single effort may be in itself.

To leave man's fate in the hands of the so-called leaders of national governments is to commit suicide. If man is to be saved, man must save himself.

No one who realizes this and attempts to arouse individual

men and women to action need apologize for making the effort.

The reader will find relatively little in this book about the external enemies of Western civilization. This is not because the author underrates the lethal threat posed by aggressive communist imperialism. It is because the author believes that communist imperialism derives its ability to pose a lethal threat chiefly from the failures of Western policy; and that these failures, in turn, derive from certain perceivable and probably curable weaknesses within the Western community of nations.

Hence the major emphasis in this study lies upon an attempt to analyze the West itself rather than its enemies, in the hope of shedding some small light upon what are the major Western weaknesses and how perhaps they may be remedied before it is too late.

JAMES P. WARBURG

Greenwich, Connecticut

POSTSCRIPT

This book was already on the press when Secretary of State John Foster Dulles was tragically stricken with a recurrence of the malady against which he had so bravely battled for the past two years. Although the writer has expressed in the pages a sharp dissent from some of Mr. Dulles' policies, he wishes to pay sincere tribute to the courage, the indefatigable vigor and the selfless devotion with which he has served the country during a trying and difficult time. It is sadly ironical that he should have been incapacitated at the very moment when it appeared that he was about to exert his powerful influence in leading the West toward greater flexibility.

J.P.W.

CONTENTS

THE WEST IN CRISIS

CHAPTER ONE

How Civilized Is Our Civilization?

I

You and I belong to that segment of the human family which, for want of a better term, is commonly referred to as "Western Man." This somewhat misleading designation is applied to that small minority of the world's population which first gathered in the eastern Mediterranean basin, spread from there over most of Europe, settled the two Americas, the southern tip of Africa and the antipodes, establishing in these widely separated regions of the earth something of a common way of life which we call "Western civilization."

Western Man is accustomed to ascendancy. He thinks of himself as having brought civilization to its highest point. Both his ascendancy and the hypothesis upon which it rests are now on trial.

Racially, there is no such thing as Western Man. The Mediterranean basin was originally populated by peoples of many racial and tribal strains. Over the centuries, Western Man has conquered and absorbed, and been conquered and influenced by many other ethnic groups, including Goths, Vandals, African Negroes, and American Indians. Western civilization is not a white civilization by any means, but it is strongly permeated by the notion of white supremacy. Because of this notion, the community of Western Man is divided within itself and, because of it, the influence of Western civilization has been impaired. If we ask ourselves why the majority of mankind is apparently in-different to the survival of Western civilization, a part of the answer lies in Western Man's assumption that he is somehow superior to other human beings because of the lighter pigmentation of his skin.

But that is not the whole answer.

For the past five centuries at least, Western Man has dominated the course of world history. Western Man originally acquired his ascendancy because he gained a head start over the rest of mankind in the struggle against his physical environment.

Western Man's material heritage derived from many earlier Mediterranean civilizations, such as those of the Persians, Egyptians, Phoenicians, and of course the Greeks and Romans. These peoples were the first to emancipate themselves from the shackles of a primitive nomadic or agricultural subsistence economy, to discover the division of labor, to learn how to trade, to manufacture, to accumulate capital, and to achieve mobility over land and sea.

Through his more rapid material progress, Western Man was able to acquire more and more relative military and economic power and also more and more relative knowledge and freedom.

Western Man's spiritual heritage derived from Judaism, from the humanism of the ancient Greeks, and from the teachings of Jesus Christ. Judaism gave Western Man the concept of a single, universal God and of a human society based upon justice under God's law. Greece gave Western Man the belief in the human individual as a rational being and, hence, the concepts of freedom of thought, freedom of expression, and political democracy. Judaism, however, embodied a contradiction between belief in a single, universal God and a religious setting in which that God appeared as the God of only a single, chosen people. Christianity resolved this contradiction by its assertion of the brotherhood of man, from which flowed its teaching of brotherly love, compassion, and non-violent resistance to aggression.

Our civilization has for centuries practiced neither the Jewish teaching of justice under moral law nor the Greek teaching of rational thought and behavior, and least of all the Christian teaching of love, compassion, and human brotherhood. Since the birth of Christ, the West has produced no great apostle of non-violence equivalent to Mahatma Gandhi. Our civilization has spawned crusaders, inquisitors, conquerors, and tyrants—Torquemadas, Napoleons, Hitlers, and Stalins—but not a single great prophet of brotherhood and peace.

The Western world, which we like to think of as "the cradle of civilization," has been the breeding ground of most of the fratricidal conflicts with which the human race has been afflicted for the past two thousand years.

The fatal weaknesses of Western Man have been his insatiable acquisitiveness and his inability to live at peace with himself. Both are the products of a materialism insufficiently restrained by humanitarianism and moral sensibility. The component parts of Western society did not unite in order to guide mankind toward progress in peace and justice. They quarreled ceaselessly among each other over their religious dogmas, their possessions, and their opportunities for aggrandizement. They fought over the hegemony of Europe, over the ownership of newly discovered parts of the world, and, finally, over the domination of the world itself.

In his endless quarrels, Western Man has reached forever more deadly weapons of murder and destruction. His moral sense has been more and more subordinated to expediency and to false concepts of patriotism. In World War I it was still considered a moral atrocity to bombard an open city with long-range artillery. In World War II scarcely a moral protest was raised against thousand-bomber raids upon sleeping cities. Today a single plane or missile can carry more destruction than was inflicted by all the air raids of World War II. Every hour of day and night, planes or missiles, each carrying this lethal load, are ready, at a moment's notice, to slay innocent millions and to make the earth uninhabitable for the human race.

Ironically, Western Man, in his materialism unrestrained by moral scruple, has now all but destroyed the foundations of his own supremacy. In so far as his ascendancy rested upon superior force of arms, he has developed weapons to the point where they have become useless as a means of enforcing his will. To the extent that his power was economic, he has wasted his strength in fratricidal conflict. Where his advantage derived from knowledge and skill not possessed by other peoples, his own inventions have so reduced time and distance as to make the maintenance of his monopoly impossible. Where Western Man might have gained the respect and admiration of the masses of mankind through empathetic understanding and co-operation, he has undermined his own influence by his selfishness, his callous inhumanity, and his failure to live up to the moral standards of the religious beliefs which he so militantly proselytized.

Thus Western Man missed his great opportunity to establish what might have been a world leadership based upon consent rather than conquest.

II

In contrast to the materialistic development of Western civilization, most of the great Asian civilizations turned inward, emphasizing man's spiritual development rather than his material progress. Some authorities say that this was due to the inherently different nature of Eastern Man. Others maintain that this view puts the cart before the horse—that Eastern Man turned inward because his harsh physical environment compelled him to seek solace in contemplation. Whatever the original cause, it is a fact that in most Asian societies the study of the past, the observance of family, tribal, caste, or religious customs, and the contemplation of man's nature and his relation to the universe have, until very recently, overshadowed the pursuit of material progress. Broadly speaking, Eastern Man has for the past five hundred years been passive and non-aggressive by comparison with Western Man's aggressive activity.

Under the impact of the Asian revolution, this pattern is rapidly changing, most markedly in China.

Africa is only a step or two behind Asia. Africa and Asia contain two thirds of the world's population.

Most students of history would agree that Tsarist Russia belonged to the Western world, even though it had been subjected to Asian influence and, geographically, was as much a part of Asia as of Europe. Tsarist Russia was one of the European powers which quarreled among each other for centuries over dynastic rights and territorial possessions; it bore its share of responsibility for World War I. Tsarist Russia's Asian empire was essentially no different from the colonial empire of Britain, except that it was not separated from the mother country by water; part of it had been acquired by conquest and part by Russian settlement of relatively empty Siberian space.

Tsarist Russia was a devoutly Christian country. Its cultural heritage, though not identical with that of Europe, was certainly more like it than like that of its Asian neighbors.

But what of Soviet Russia?

Karl Marx was a German. *Das Kapital* was written in the British Museum. Communism, as now practiced in the Soviet Union, is a distorted offshoot of West European socialism. Like socialism, it originated as a protest against nineteenth-century capitalism and exploitative imperialism.

However, since the Bolshevik Revolution, Soviet leadership has increasingly turned its back upon the West, orienting itself more and more toward Asia. The Soviet Union is now a multi-national state rather than a European nation with a colonial empire in Asia. In some respects this multi-national state is more Asian than European. Soviet leadership has rejected Christianity and has adopted a theory of the relationship of the individual to the state which is antithetical to the Western concept.

Soviet Man has detached himself from the West. He conceives of Western Man as his enemy, yet the materialistic standards by which he measures his accomplishments are largely the materialistic standards of the West. Soviet Man challenges Western Man with the latter's own weapons. Together with Western Man, he stands on trial before mankind, on the charge of holding the entire human race at the brink of destruction. Against this indictment Soviet Man can plead that it was not he who opened the door into the atomic age and that, unlike Western Man, he has not yet used a single nuclear weapon.

The fact is that Soviet Man has adopted our own crass materialism and added to it an explicit repudiation of the moral restraints in which we still have the grace to profess belief.

We have betrayed the Judaeo-Christian heritage. Soviet Man has rejected it altogether.

III

The dawn of the atomic age robbed physical power of its significance as an instrument of rational policy. Yet Western Man and Soviet Man have entered upon a struggle for preponderance of physical power, as if neither of them realized what has occurred.

To describe the so-called nuclear stalemate by the simile of two scorpions in a bottle ignores the all-important fact that if the two great antagonists annihilate each other they will also kill off the human race. Yet this fact embraces the entire significance of the situation we face. This fact draws a line between the nuclear antagonists and the rest of humanity, making pariahs of the nuclear powers.

Logically the nuclear stalemate should provide a guarantee against race suicide. But the history of man does not follow the course of logic. History is written more by accident than design, often by the wholly irrational acts of madmen.

Fear is the great enemy of reason. Fear lest the madman, Hitler, produce an atomic weapon led the Anglo-Saxon democracies to open the Pandora's Box of atomic weaponry. Fear drove Stalin to desperate efforts to break the American monopoly. Fear produced the American H-bomb and its Soviet counterpart.

There is no answer to fear except in the realm of the spirit. Where moral conscience is submerged by materialistic expediency, fear inevitably creates hatred and the impulse toward aggression; and the desire to kill an enemy creates the need to believe that the enemy is so wholly evil that he deserves to be killed in the name of righteousness. There is no older story than this in the history of Western Man. Only now the conventional ending is no longer possible. Murder has become automatically punishable by suicide.

We know all this, and so do the Russians. Yet the scorpions are twisting and turning in the bottle.

Soviet leadership cherishes the illusion that the banning of nuclear weapons could restore the old order, in which the communists' massive conventional armaments would leave them supreme. Western leadership chases the mirage of a "limited nuclear war"—a war in which the Russians would graciously permit us to use just enough nuclear weapons to offset their conventional superiority. Each in its own way is trying to turn back the clock of history and thus to obtain an advantage over the other.

But history refuses to be reversed. Inventions cannot be uninvented. *The price which history demands for a safe-conduct into the atomic age is not the limitation and control of armaments but the abolition of war.*

Meanwhile, mankind trembles in apprehension, looking with mounting incomprehension and resentment at the two irresponsible antagonists. Soon China, with one quarter of the world's population, will enter upon the scene as a third and wholly unpredictable element.

The world knows that we of the West began this madness and looks to us to end it. This is easier said than done, but it must be done if the human race is to survive. *How* it can be done is one of the major topics to be discussed in this study.

IV

The cold war is essentially a struggle for the allegiance of the majority of mankind—a struggle between two different concepts of the nature of man and of man's relationship to his fellow man, to his country, and to the universe. It is true that this conflict involves a clash of social-economic theories, but the antithesis between "capitalism" and "socialism" is more apparent than real. The West is no longer capitalist in the Marxist sense, and certainly the communist system is nearer to state capitalism than to socialism. Nor can the struggle be accurately described as a conflict between democracy and dictatorship. The communist orbit provides certain elements of freedom not hitherto enjoyed by its inhabitants. The West has its enclaves of tyranny and dictatorship.

The real essence of the conflict is between two kinds of governments—between governments which foster revolutionary change in what they conceive to be their nations' interests without regard to any concept of international morality, and governments whose policies and actions in support of the *status quo* are limited and guided—no matter how imperfectly—by the moral concept of their peoples.

This antithesis remains obscured so long as both sides pursue the morally indefensible policy of threatening nuclear war.

Such a policy is perhaps consistent with the Marxist-Leninist philosophy, in which violence is sanctioned as an instrument of promoting revolution. It is wholly inconsistent with the professed philosophy of the West.

The Western policy of nuclear deterrence assumes that the risks of nuclear war are preferable to any substantial further expansion of the Sino-Soviet orbit. Underlying this assumption is a tacit belief that race suicide is preferable to a communist conquest of the world. Apart from the fact that this attitude poses a wholly false choice of alternatives, what right have we of the West to make any such choice for all of humanity? Even if we assume that most of the English-speaking peoples and some of the European and Latin-American peoples would find life intolerable under communist dictatorship, how true is this of those great masses of humanity who have never had a taste of freedom? By what moral authority are we entitled to threaten nuclear war—which means extinction for most if not all of humanity—in order to prevent the communists from seizing two little islands off the coast of Asia?

Until the West recaptures its lost moral sensibility, its struggle against communism will remain all but meaningless to the majority of mankind.

V

When and if the threat of race suicide is removed, it will become apparent that the real tension in the world exists not so much between Western Man and Sino-Soviet Man as between the privileged and underprivileged—between the peoples seeking to preserve what they possess and the peoples seeking change for the better.

Except for certain enclaves of poverty, notably in Latin America, the peoples of the Western world live in relative comfort and abundance, while the vast majority of the human race exists in varying degrees of misery. In the past this has been taken more or less for granted, much as the supposedly immutable fate of "the poor" was until recent times taken for granted within Western society.

If the world is saved from destruction, it will no longer be a world in which gross inequality and injustice will be tolerated. The hitherto underpriviledged peoples are on the march.

If Western Man wishes to survive, he will have to learn—and learn very quickly—how to live in and with a world which has forever escaped from his control—a world suddenly freed from the fetters of ignorance and released from the coercion of superior physical power.

Western Man will have to do more than endeavor to compete successfully with the communist dictatorships in extending aid to the emerging peoples. He will have to give humanistic meaning to the material assistance he offers. He will have to recapture his belief in the brotherhood of man and rediscover the forgotten teachings of love and compassion. He will have to devote his resources and his ingenuity to the establishment of worldwide social justice as an end in itself—not as a measure of defense against a communist adversary.

Without a reawakening of Western morality, it is extremely doubtful whether Western Man can, in fact, compete successfully with the communists.

The communists' power of attraction derives from their nearness to poverty—from the fact that they have only recently lifted themselves out of illiteracy and squalid backwardness. Thus they have set an example which seems to the emerging peoples relevant to their own predicament and capable of emulation, whereas the high living standards and the accouterments of Western civilization seem out of reach and irrelevant.

Western Man can offset this disadvantage only by greater empathetic understanding of the needs and aspirations of peoples on the march toward what they hope will be a better future, by greater concern for universal social justice as well as for political freedom, by greater respect for divergent belief and opinion—in short, by making love and concern for humanity the operative factors in place of retentiveness and fear.

If our civilization is overrun and submerged by the global revolution of the underprivileged, it will be chiefly because we have failed to learn humility—because we have failed to recognize that we of the West are in no intrinsic sense superior or entitled to special privilege. This is going to be a difficult lesson for Western Man to learn. Notions such as "white supremacy" or *la mission civilisatrice* do not die easily; nor do the habits of greed, possessiveness, and lust for power.

VI

If this is the nature of the crisis of Western Man, we must ask ourselves several questions:

Why have we been sleepwalking into disaster?

How has this crisis come upon us?

What is it that our enemies seek to destroy and that we wish to preserve and defend?

In answer to the last question, most inhabitants of the Western world would probably reply:

"Political freedom, economic freedom, and freedom of worship." The order in which these three elements would be stated as well as the words used to describe them might vary, but the essence of the answer would remain the same.

If asked to define the existing threat or threats to these cherished attributes of Western civilization, most inhabitants of the Western world would probably think at once of an external menace. The simplest and most likely answer would be: "Communism."

The main thesis of this book is that, while the external threat exists, the mortal danger to Western civilization is not the enemy without but the enemy within the gates; that the political and economic systems of the West are being eroded from within; and that the external threat to Western civilization arises less from the strength of its would-be destroyers than from the weakness of its defenders.

In order to develop this thesis, the succeeding chapters will deal: first, with Western political democracy; then with the economic system of the West, commonly and somewhat inaccurately referred to as "free-enterprise capitalism"; then with the political dilemma of the West in a rapidly and radically changing world; and finally with some aspects of Western Man's conditioning by his political, economic, and cultural environment.

Although this study attempts to examine the Western community as a whole, it inevitably focuses in large measure upon the United States—partly because the author is an American, but even more because, for better or worse, the United States has been cast by contemporary history in the role of the leading defender of Western civilization. Thus the chapter entitled "Threats to 'Capitalism'" is followed by "Soft Spots in the American Economy," and this in turn leads to a discussion of the great economic opportunity which was lost by the United States in the first postwar decade. Similarly, in dealing with the postwar political problems encountered by the West, the spotlight tends to fall mostly upon United States foreign policy, since the decisions reached or not reached in Washington have been so largely responsible for both the successes and failures of the West in this period of history.

The reader may perhaps feel that the emphasis throughout this study lies somewhat too heavily upon Western failures; yet the incontrovertible fact remains that we are no nearer to peace than we were when World War II ended, and that the specter of World War III looms over the human race more ominously now than at any time since 1945.

Finally, if this study conveys any compressible "message," it is that the foreign policy of a nation or group of nations is conditioned less by the "decisions" of those in high office than by the internal nature and behavior of the societies which those in high office represent; and that the survival or demise of Western civilization will be determined more by such internal matters as the regulation of monopolies, the treatment of minorities, and the nature of the educational system than by the arts of external diplomacy.

The decline of the West is undeniable, but in the writer's opinion it is by no means irreversible. The renaissance of Western civilization must begin within Western society. The key element in Western society is Individual Man.

CHAPTER TWO

Democracy on Trial

I

When President Wilson, during World War I, adopted the slogan of making the world "safe for democracy," he was in effect expressing the belief that the existence of what was then called "autocracy" anywhere in the world constituted a mortal threat to the existence of democracy.

The fact is, however, that since the days of Pericles more democratic governments have fallen of their own weakness than have been overthrown by foreign tyrants, kings, or dictators. One thinks, of course, of such recent contrary examples as Spain and Czechoslovakia, but as against these there is a much longer list of democratic governments overturned by internal revolution. After World War I, republics or constitutional monarchies succumbed to dictatorship in Italy, Greece, Rumania, Hungary, Austria, Weimar Germany, Portugal, and Spain (before Franco), without foreign intervention. Perón overturned the Argentine Republic, and democracy has yielded to dictatorship from time to time in Latin-American republics too numerous to mention. Actually, it was not until Hitler and Mussolini helped Francisco Franco to power that foreign intervention played any important part in destroying democratic governments. It is true that dictatorship is the enemy of democracy, but democracy's most deadly enemy is its own all-too-frequent failure to live up to its promise of social justice and equal opportunity.

27

Economic and social democracy do not automatically accompany the establishment of universal suffrage and representative government.

II

Many factors influence the success or failure of democracy, such as the level of literacy and education, the presence or absence of natural resources, the historical background and the innate attitude of a people toward freedom, security, and individual responsibility. Because of the varying size and nature of the political and economic units of the Western world, it is impossible to generalize, except perhaps to this extent:

Democracy can work successfully only when the majority of individual citizens understand the questions to be decided by their government and are able to recognize how and why they want these questions to be decided.

In the world of today, a number of factors work against the fulfillment of this condition.

Mere size, in area and population, is one such condition. It is obviously easier for four million Finns to understand and deal with their country's problems—even when they include the difficult problem of dealing with a powerful, anti-democratic neighbor—than it is for 180 million citizens of the United States.

Economic diversification, desirable though it be for other reasons, multiplies and complicates the problems of democratic government. And when technology, mass production, and monopoly enter upon the scene, the individual citizen is so far removed from the decision-making process that he finds it almost impossible to participate in it.

Take, for example, the development of democracy in the United States. When the Founding Fathers wrote the American Constitution, they were dealing with thirteen colonies along the Atlantic seaboard with a combined population of about four million. Slaves, women, minors, and non-property-owners were excluded from the franchise. Of the remainder entitled to vote, nearly all were either farmers, land speculators, merchants, small manufacturers, or shopkeepers. Each one of these "small businessmen," unless he was an isolated frontiersman, knew, or at least thought he knew, what was good or bad for his business and hence what he wished the government to do or not to do. Contrast this with the United States as it is today—a country in which production and distribution are concentrated in a handful of giant corporate enterprises employing the vast majority of the working population—a country in which the small businessman is rapidly disappearing and in which the working force does its bargaining collectively through huge trade or industrial unions.

The formation of national policy has become a complicated process of finding compromises between a multiplicity of conflicting interests and of weighing one risk against another. The small businessman, the individual entrepreneur, was familiar with bargaining his interest against that of another. He was accustomed to weighing and taking risks. How is the man on the assembly line or the white-collar employee in the office staff of General Motors or the dealer who sells General Motors cars to know whether Engine-Charlie Wilson spoke truth or falsehood when he declared, as a government servant, that "what's good for General Motors is good for the country"? How is he even to know what is good for General Motors? How, as a citizen, is he enabled to weigh risks, when the major risks that affect his life—except the risk of losing his job through incompetence—are risks taken for him, concerning which he has no knowledge and over which he has no control?

In a recent study undertaken for the Fund for the Republic, Professor Andrew Hacker of Cornell University points out: "The corporation has certainly not set out to weaken the foundations of democratic politics, but its growth as the characteristic institution of our time is having this consequence." Speaking of what he calls the new "middle-middle class" of corporate employees, he finds that most of these citizens renounce politics either out of fear of jeopardizing their careers or because "being non-political becomes an aspect of their personalities." Moreover, Professor Hacker believes that "impersonal corporate interests are replacing personal interests as the concern of politicians."

There can be no doubt that the growth of a highly concentrated machine-age society tends to alienate the individual citizen from the process of policy formation essential to the successful functioning of a democracy.

It is true that the citizen can, by joining pressure groups, exercise a certain amount of influence. This will be discussed in a later chapter. But even within a pressure group, such as a labor union or a trade association, the individual tends to become lost as an individual, leaving the defense of his interest to professional leadership.

This tendency might perhaps be offset if the increased leisure provided by the ever greater automation of production and distribution were put to use in deliberately planned education for citizenship. There is as yet no indication of any such development. To the extent that the American citizen devotes any part of his leisure time to citizenship, he devotes it to local community affairs, which he can understand and which have a direct and visible bearing upon his daily life. This makes for more effective democracy at the local level, but it fails to arrest the degeneration of democracy at the national level.

III

Another major threat to political democracy lies in its growing incompetence to deal with the problems of the nation-state in a world in which the sovereignty of the nation-state is unrestricted by superior authority.

It has long been obvious that there can be no durable peace in a world of international anarchy; that a world order without world law is an anachronism; and that, since war now means the extinction of civilization, a world which fails to establish the rule of law over the nation-states cannot long continue to exist.

We are living in a perilous period of transition from the era of the fully sovereign nation-state to the era of world government. No one knows how long the period of transition will last, nor whether it will end in the firm establishment of peace or in race suicide.

But we do know this: So long as the state of international anarchy continues, the democracies will be at a terrifying disadvantage as against hostile dictatorships.

Alexis de Tocqueville foresaw this difficulty in his *Democracy in America,* written in 1835. Here is what he said:

> Foreign politics demand scarcely any of those qualities which are peculiar to a democracy; they require, on the contrary, the perfect use of almost all those in which it is deficient. A democracy can only with great difficulty regulate the details of an important undertaking, persevere in a fixed design and work out its execution in spite of serious obstacles. It cannot combine its measures with secrecy or await their consequences with patience . . . Almost all the defects inherent in democratic institutions are brought to light in the conduct of foreign affairs; their advantages are less perceptible.

During the period of transition in which we are living, democracy will be threatened *from within* because the peoples of the democracies will tend to become dissatisfied with governments which are continuously outmarched and outmaneuvered by the hostile dictatorships. The individual citizen will feel increasingly frustrated and thus more and more susceptible to the appeal of a would-be leader who promises, if given complete authority, to remedy the evil.

The way to meet this danger is easy enough to see but hard to follow: democratic governments, if they intend to survive these perilous times, must acquire greater flexibility, more imagination, and a clearer vision of the future in competing with hostile dictatorships. Above all, they must develop both a greater responsiveness to popular opinion and a greater ability to inform and educate the broad masses.

IV

A variant of what has happened in other democracies—Italy, Weimar Germany, or the Fourth French Republic—can happen to any democracy in which the people become dissatisfied with their government's inability to remedy what seems to them an intolerable situation, forgetting—because they have become alienated from the processes of policy formation—that their government's failure is their own failure.

In this respect the British parliamentary system embodies a useful safeguard in that it provides the people with the means of changing an administration whenever they have lost confidence in it. It is true that Parliament does not always immediately reflect majority popular opinion by a vote of no confidence, thus forcing a general election; but it does so often enough and, as a rule, quickly enough, to keep the people aware of the fact that the government is their government.

It is misleading, however, to place too much emphasis upon the constitutional machinery of democracy. For example, it is widely believed that the Fourth French Republic decayed and died primarily because the constitution of 1946 created an all-powerful legislature and a weak executive—a defect for which a remedy is now being sought through constitutional reform. Anglo-Saxon observers usually add that "the French have been unable to govern themselves because they have never given up their factionalism in favor of a two-party system." Both of these allegations no doubt contain an element of truth, but they fail to go to the root of the matter.

The Fourth Republic died, as many democracies have died, because the French people lost interest in and a sense of responsibility for their government, leaving it in the hands of a small group of professional politicians, surrounded on the left by the communists and on the right by the extreme reactionaries. Most of these middle-of-the-road politicians were swayed by petty personal ambition or by the influence of various conflicting special-interest groups. The lobby representing the settlers, investors, and speculators in the French colonial empire became disproportionately powerful because it attracted the tacit support of that part of almost every Frenchman which is still deeply moved by nostalgic memories of past glory. The powerful influence of the colonial lobby prevented France from coming to terms with the world-wide anti-colonial revolution, forcing the nation into an attempt to suppress by force the rebellions in

Indochina and North Africa. These colonial wars bankrupted the French treasury, weakened the French position in Europe, especially as against a resurgent Germany, and finally alienated the French officer corps from a "system" which had humiliated the army in Indochina and could neither settle the war in North Africa nor win it. Thus the stage was set for the re-emergence of an authoritarian leader.

Even this brief and necessarily superficial analysis, which ignores the historical background of French politics and the peculiar factors which affected postwar France, will suffice to demonstrate the relative unimportance of the defects of the French constitution under the Fourth Republic.

A constitutionally strong presidency and a two-party system will not necessarily insure the working of political democracy, as witness the condition prevailing in the United States at this critical moment of world history. A constitutionally strong executive can be rendered impotent by a weak incumbent. A two-party system can be distorted into an arrangement under which both parties pursue essentially the same policy, each claiming credit for what is good in that policy and blaming the other for what is bad. If the policy fails, both parties are tarred with its failure. Since the so-called opposition has presented no alternative program, the people are left with nothing to vote *for* in place of what they know they are against.

Any system of democratic government works only when the voters are given not merely an opportunity to express a preference for personalities but a preference for one program of action as against another. This is the function of a two-party system. In the absence of a clearly presented choice of alternative policies and programs of action, elections in a democracy become little more than popularity contests in which personal charm plays a greater part than qualification for high office. This is the road which readily leads to the point where an anxiety-ridden people will confide its destiny into the hands of a father-figure. If the people are unlucky in their choice, they may find out too late that they have elected an impotent figurehead or enthroned a dictator.

V

Democracy is more than a system of government. It is a way of communal life conceived and developed by mature men in an essentially middle-class society seeking to free themselves from the parental authority of an overlord.

For this very reason, democracy cannot be successfully imitated by an immature people. To expect Egypt, for example, to leap straight from feudalism into democracy is to expect the impossible. Egypt had to have its Nasser, just as Turkey had to have its Atatürk, before it could move toward representative government. The Western nations do democracy and themselves a disservice when they encourage the premature adoption of democratic forms by emerging peoples historically or economically unprepared for self-government. Indonesia, Burma, and Pakistan are examples.

But, if the adoption of democracy requires political maturity, its preservation demands the perpetuation of certain youthful qualities. Democracy cannot be preserved by a people grown feeble or indolent with age or irresponsible with too easily gained and too long sustained prosperity. Democracy cannot be preserved where anxiety to preserve the *status quo* has supplanted the spirit of adventure. For democracy *is* adventure. Once it identifies itself with the past, or even with the present, it goes inevitably into decline.

VI

It was said a moment ago that democracy is essentially the product of a mature middle-class society; that is to say, a society in which the dominant elements have an interest in individual property ownership and in the pursuit of profit. "No taxation without representation" was the demand of an essentially middle-class American colonial society.

In recent times perhaps the greatest enemy of a middle-class society—and, therefore, the greatest enemy of Western democracy—has been inflation. It is extremely doubtful whether Hitler would ever have come to power in Germany had not the inflation of the German currency first destroyed the middle class and undermined the strength of the Weimar Republic. Fascism and communism both breed most readily where the middle class either does not exist or where it is weakened or wiped out by debasement of the currency and the consequent destruction of savings. This very real threat to Western democracy will be more fully discussed in subsequent chapters.

VII

The challenge to Western democracy, stated in broad terms, is political, socio-economic, and moral.

The political challenge is to overcome the dehumanizing effects of the technological revolution, so that Individual Man may recapture his individuality in a world of machines and mechanical brains and thus regain his ability to function as a responsible, self-governing citizen.

The social-economic challenge to democracy is to demonstrate that it is not necessary to sacrifice political freedom and the dignity of Individual Man in order to achieve social justice; or, stated in other terms, to show that it is possible in a middle-class society to harness the pursuit of profit to the greatest good of the greatest number.

The moral challenge to democracy is to rid itself of the cancer of racial or religious discrimination; to dissociate itself from colonial exploitation and from expedient alliances with anti-democratic forces; and to associate itself firmly with the aspirations of all men everywhere seeking human betterment under justice, dignity, and freedom.

Unless Western civilization meets this threefold challenge, it is quite conceivable that Western civilization might perish and that democracy might still survive, as a gift bequeathed by a dying civilization to its successors. For Western civilization to survive along with democracy—perhaps its greatest gift to man—it is necessary for the Western community to identify *itself*, as well as the concept of political freedom, with the irresistible march of mankind into the future.

CHAPTER THREE

Threats to "Capitalism"

I

The economic system of the West, if such it can be called, is, like the Western political system, threatened by external and internal dangers.

Although Western leadership was originally slow to recognize the economic threat of communism owing to its obsession with the military aspect, awareness of communist economic strength and of the competitive advantages enjoyed by communist dictatorships now overshadows and obscures the equally serious dangers which threaten the Western economic structure from within. For this reason an examination of these internal dangers may be appropriate.

Actually there is no such thing as an economic system of the West. The Western community includes *laissez-faire* economies, mixed economies, and state-controlled economies. It includes a few countries in which nineteenth-century, dog-eat-dog capitalism still prevails; countries in which the pursuit of private profit has been so regulated in the interest of the general welfare that Karl Marx would not recognize them as "capitalist"; and countries in which avowedly socialist governments control a greater part of economic life than private enterprise.

"The West" is not an economic unit. It is an aggregation of large, medium-sized, and small units, each pursuing its own ends. Most of these units are single nation-states. A few consist of loosely co-ordinated groups of nation-states, such as the British Commonwealth or Benelux or the nations of Western Europe attempting to achieve a "common market."

The diversity of the Western economies is not necessarily a weakness, though it presents problems. But a serious weakness lies in the fact that the component units of the Western economic structure behave toward each other in a way which at times resembles the behavior of individuals in a primitive capitalist society; that is to say, each unit pursues its own interests without regard for the interests of others.

Efforts have been made, with varying success, to regulate and soften economic competition and to establish something like a code of fair practices, but on the whole the nation-states have shown themselves as unwilling to limit their economic sovereignty as they have been reluctant to yield any part of their political sovereignty in the interests of peace.

Paradoxically, war has produced greater co-operation among the nations of the West than peace. Lend-Lease is an outstanding example. The Marshall Plan, as originally conceived, was an exception, but its actual operation, after the Kremlin had declined to participate, was chiefly inspired by common fear of a common enemy.

It is equally paradoxical that fear of war has also been the primary cause of the economic anarchy which has plagued the Western world. Fear of war drove nations to seek economic self-sufficiency in order to free themselves from dependence upon foreign sources of supply. Tariffs, quotas, and exchange controls were used to stimulate domestic production and to protect it against foreign competition.

The quest for economic self-sufficiency invariably starts a vicious circle. One nation's imports are the exports of other nations. When one nation reduces its imports for the sake of stimulating home production, it deprives other nations of a market in which to sell their surplus products. A nation which cannot export its surplus goods soon finds itself unable to buy the surplus goods of other nations and is thus compelled to restrict its own imports. And so it goes. One barrier to the natural flow of trade provokes the erection of another, until practically

37

all of international trade is strangled. The strangulation of trade creates hardship everywhere and engenders resentment. . . . This is what led up to the Great Depression in the period between the two world wars. For fear of being cut off from essential supplies in the event of war, the nations of the West embarked upon a course of economic action almost certain to provoke war.

Today the Western nations realize that economic self-sufficiency is no longer attainable because, in this shrunken world, all the nations have become interdependent, especially those with highly developed and complex industrial structures. But the same restrictive devices are still being used, not to seek an illusory self-sufficiency, but to seek the individual advantage of one nation over others. The result is different only in degree.

The Western community of nations will be dangerously weak so long as these anarchic practices continue. It will be weak both in terms of its inner health and in terms of the grim competition it must face from the highly integrated communist orbit.

II

Eventually the goal of Western economic policy must be to bring about world-wide economic co-operation in place of cutthroat competition. But world-wide economic co-operation cannot be achieved until the political tensions are eliminated or at least substantially reduced.

So long as the world remains divided into two mutually hostile blocs of nations, with a third bloc either maintaining a watchful neutrality or playing off one side against the other, the economic problems of the West are best considered in three separate though related parts. These are: (1) Western internal economic relations; (2) Western relations with the uncommitted nations; and (3) Western economic relations with the communist orbit.

1. INTRA-WESTERN ECONOMIC RELATIONS

(a) *Latin America*

Many students of foreign affairs, among them this observer,

have warned in the past against taking Latin America's adherence to the Western community for granted, pointing out how continued neglect of Latin-American interests and susceptibilities might lead to its alienation. Unfortunately it was apparently necessary that a high United States official and his wife be spat upon and stoned during what was intended to be a friendly visit to Latin America before Western leaders could be shaken out of their complacency. It remains to be seen whether this unhappy incident will be forgotten or serve to arouse awareness that Latin America is both politically and economically vital to the Western community.

The twenty republics have a combined population about equal to that of the United States, estimated to be among the world's most rapidly growing population groups. Aboriginal Indians and the descendants of African Negroes form a large part of this population; in some countries they are in the majority. In view of the arrested development of race relations in the United States and in view of *apartheid* in South Africa, the West can disclaim being "a white man's club" only if it fully integrates Latin America into the Western community. This is of crucial importance in shaping Western relations with the mostly non-white peoples of Asia, Africa, and the Middle East.

Compared to the peoples of the North Atlantic basin, Latin-Americans as a whole live at an extremely low level of income, health, and education. In some countries, illiteracy runs as high as 80 per cent. In many, life expectancy at birth is not much over thirty years. Per capita annual income runs from about four hundred dollars in the Argentine, Uruguay, and Cuba to less than one hundred dollars in much of Central America. Throughout most of the area there is a wide gap between the wealthy few and the multitudinous poor. The West can deny the allegation that the Atlantic community is "a rich man's club" only if it brings Latin America into full partnership. This, too, is vitally important in its effect upon Western relations with the have-not peoples of Asia and Africa.

Apart from these political considerations, the raw-material wealth of Latin America and its potential as a market for manufactured goods make it essential to the economy of the West. Given the proper care, attention, and assistance, the southern half of the Western Hemisphere can mean to the Western community of nations what the North American West has meant to the development of the United States and Canada.

Like the emerging peoples of Asia and Africa, the Latin Americans are seeking to achieve in a few short years the economic and technological status of Western Europe and North America without having either the experience or the capital accumulated by Europe and North America over the centuries. Culturally and geographically the Latin-Americans belong to the West, but if they fail to obtain effective help from the more developed members of the Western community they will turn elsewhere and eventually cease to be members of that community.

Latin America needs more and better technical assistance, more capital investment, and a stabilization of the prices of the raw materials upon which its economic life depends. These matters can be more conveniently discussed in connection with similar aid to the uncommitted peoples. What Latin America needs most of all, however, is to be brought into the Western community as an equal and respected partner.

(b) Intra-Western Trade and Finance

As noted in an earlier section of this chapter, trade does not flow as freely as it should among the nations of the Western community, chiefly because of the shortsighted, nationalistic, and, on the whole, obsolete policies still being pursued by most of the Western nations.

A major consequence of the inhibition of trade is to deny the consumer throughout the world the benefit of the lower prices which would result from a more rational distribution of production.

A second consequence of trade restriction is to render the problem of financing the exchange of goods and services complicated and difficult.

For many years Great Britain acted as the banker for most of the world's trade. This came about partly through Britain's role as the center of a far-flung empire and as the world's largest maritime power and partly from the fact that Britain's steadily favorable trade balance (excess of exports over imports) made her the world's leading creditor nation. In order to continue, year after year, selling more to other countries than she purchased abroad, Britain found it necessary to lend money to the debtor countries or to invest permanently in their railroads, plantations, and industries. Had she not done this, the debtor countries would very soon have been unable to continue their purchases of British manufactures.

Up to about the time of World War I, the British pound sterling, convertible into gold at a fixed rate, came close to occupying the position of a world currency. The British policy of free trade and liberal foreign investment created a fairly well stabilized international balance of payments, offsetting Britain's chronically favorable balance of trade. In these circumstances it was possible for most of the nations to maintain their currencies in a fixed relationship to gold and to settle temporary deficits in their balances of payment by shipping gold. This meant that the currencies of these nations always remained convertible into gold—each at its own ratio —and hence into other gold-standard currencies.

One of the many and complicated causes of World War I was that Germany challenged Great Britain's position as the world's leading manufacturer, maritime power, and banker. Although the German challenge was defeated, World War I destroyed the system of trade and finance under which the Western community of nations had lived and, on the whole, prospered for a century. To meet the expenses of war, Britain was forced to sell most of her foreign investments and to borrow heavily; a large part of her merchant fleet was sunk; and the United States, hitherto a debtor nation, moved into Britain's former position as the world's largest creditor.

For a few years private bankers in the United States partially offset the now favorable trade balance by making extensive foreign loans and investments. But the government of the United States failed to recognize that the nation's creditor position demanded the drastic reduction of its protective tariff. In 1930 the Smoot-Hawley Act raised tariff rates to an all-time high. Thus the United States began to drain gold from other nations which were unable to sell enough of their goods in the American market to pay for what they had to purchase in dollars.

There were other factors which complicated the position after World War I, above all the Allied war debts to the United States, which the American government refused to cancel ("They hired the money, didn't they?"—President Coolidge) and which the Allies could pay only out of the reparations which they expected to collect from Germany.

For a short time Germany paid enough to preserve the fiction of Allied solvency. When Germany collapsed, the flimsy financial structure of the whole Western community began to totter.

This was the point at which the economic anarchy described earlier in this chapter assumed serious proportions. With their gold being drained away into the United States, the debtor countries had a choice between reducing their purchases in the United States or ending the convertibility of their currencies into gold. To reduce purchases in the United States was difficult, because the United States was now the major, if not the sole, source of food and other supplies needed for existence, let alone rehabilitation. To end the convertibility of currencies meant something very like a declaration of bankruptcy. When Great Britain went off the gold standard in 1931, it marked the end of an economic era.

The collapse of the Western system is generally thought to have been precipitated by the economic collapse of the United States—its supposedly strongest bulwark. But the stock market crash in the United States and the consequent calling in of American foreign loans was only the final straw. The destruction and dislocation caused by war, the foolish attempt to collect the costs of war from a vanquished enemy, and the *"sauve qui peut"* economic nationalism of the various countries had prepared the ground.

At the World Economic Conference, held at London in 1933, a last attempt was made to prop up the tottering system. It was too late. By this time the entire American economy was in such disarray that President Roosevelt—rightly or wrongly, and about this opinions differ—felt himself compelled to subordinate every other consideration to the achievement of domestic recovery. The refusal of the United States to lower its tariff, to co-operate in re-establishing currency stability, or to compromise the war debts touched off the final spasms of international anarchy.

This much, at least, of history is essential to an understanding of the current intra-Western problems of trade and finance.[1]

The rise of Hitler increased apprehension and further stimulated economic nationalism. On the other hand, the outbreak of World War II finally lifted the American economy out of its depression and started an unprecedented boom, based upon military production.

Meanwhile, the Reciprocal Trade Treaty program had initiated a downward revision of the American tariff—a revision which did not go nearly far enough but which at least constituted a start in the right direction.

Several other important lessons were learned from World War I experience. This time no impossible load of reparations was imposed upon the vanquished enemy, and the invention of the Lend-Lease formula avoided a repetition of the mistake of treating inter-Allied war loans as if they were purely commercial transactions.

After the war the Marshall Plan marked a notable advance on the part of the now more than ever powerful United States toward co-operation based upon enlightened self-interest in place of shortsighted economic nationalism.

Nevertheless, the basic problem of trade relationships within the Western community remained unsolved.

In so far as this problem is now recognized at all, it is most frequently referred to as a problem of insufficient liquidity or as the problem of the "dollar shortage." It is held that the International Monetary Fund and the European Payments Union—two postwar institutions designed to provide temporary

[1]For a fuller discussion of the developments leading up to the collapse of 1929–33 and the considerations affecting United States policy, see the author's *The Money Muddle*, Alfred Knopf, Inc., 1933.

For a more recent and perhaps more judicial analysis, see Arthur M. Schlesinger, Jr., *The Age of Roosevelt*, Vol. II (*The Coming of the New Deal*), Houghton Mifflin, 1958.

borrowing facilities—lack sufficient funds to finance the im-
balances arising from the present high level of international
trade. This analysis fails to go to the root of the matter.

The International Monetary Fund and the European Payments Union are partial substitutes for the old-fashioned gold
standard—partial, because gold shipments are still used to some
extent in settling international balances. Opponents of the gold
standard used to say that the reason it could not work was that
there was not enough gold in the world to finance the volume
of trade. There was some truth in this contention but by no
means the whole truth. The gold standard was a mechanism for
settling the *temporary* disequilibria in the international balance
of payments; as such it may have been inadequate at times
because of a shortage of gold. But the basic problem in the
inter-war period was not one of settling *temporary* disequilibria
any more than it is now. The problem was then, as it is today,
one of correcting the *permanent* factors of disequilibrium.

The fact is that most of the nations of the Western community
buy (import) more than they can pay for out of their sales
(export) to other countries. Some of the Western nations do
this out of sheer necessity, the exorbitant price of monopolistically controlled oil being a factor of considerable importance. Others do it because they spend more on luxuries or
social services than they can afford. In either case, these countries find it necessary to restrict their imports or to limit the
convertibility of their currencies.

In most of the Western countries there is a direct conflict
between the desire to maintain full employment and stable
consumption at home and the desire to maintain a stable, readily
convertible currency. It is no exaggeration to say that most of
the Western democracies are, in fact, pursuing simultaneously
two directly conflicting policies. On the one hand, they use
fiscal and monetary policy (budget, bank-rate, credit controls)
to keep prices down; in other words, as anti-inflation measures.
On the other hand, they employ tariffs, import quotas, and
subsidies to keep prices up; in other words, as inflationary
measures.

As the result of the imbalance of trade and of incongruously conflicting monetary and trade policies, only a few currencies have remained readily convertible. Holdings of gold and of the few so-called "hard" currencies, of which the United States dollar was the most important, made up the cash reserves of the various governments available for the settlement of international balances of payment.

The British pound sterling, though not freely convertible, remained the chief medium of exchange in the so-called Sterling Area, comprising most of the Commonwealth countries, Scandinavia, and part of the Middle East. Even though Britain managed with great difficulty to maintain a surplus of exports over imports, London continued to finance about 40 per cent of world trade; but, in spite of the most careful management, British cash reserves were dangerously inadequate. Any seasonal drain or sudden emergency, like that caused by the Suez crisis of 1956, brought the threat of financial disaster. Britain was like a private banker habitually transacting a larger business than his capital warranted.

In 1958 the Bank of England's precarious position was spectacularly eased by the fall in world prices for raw materials, caused in large measure by the economic recession in the United States. This favorable change in "the terms of trade" reduced the cost of Britain's imports and enabled her to pile up her first substantial export surplus in the postwar period, thus increasing cash reserves to the point at which it became possible to make the pound sterling more freely convertible for foreign holders.

Simultaneously, in the last days of 1958, the de Gaulle government decided to devalue the French franc and to make the new "heavy franc" convertible into gold. The European Payments Union was abolished and the European Monetary Agreement provided for the settlement of international balances in gold.

It is too soon, as this book goes to press, to form any judgment as to the effectiveness or permanence of these steps toward full convertibility.

The de Gaulle government has undertaken heavy overseas commitments which it can hope to fulfill only if it succeeds in quickly bringing about a peaceful settlement in Algeria, and then only at the price of severe domestic austerity which the French people may or may not be willing to endure.

The favorable terms of trade which Britain enjoyed in 1958 —largely at the expense of the Commonwealth suppliers of raw materials—may not be permanent. And London's financial security is heavily dependent upon continued revenues from Persian Gulf oil and upon continued willingness of the hitherto friendly Sheik of Kuwait to invest his huge annual royalties in British securities. Should Britain lose control over Kuwait, she will face a serious financial crisis. In the long run, British liquidity probably presents a problem for which a solution remains to be found.

The basic difficulty, however, lies elsewhere than in the monetary field. It lies in the fact that the two most important creditor nations in the Western community—the United States and West Germany—have not been fully functioning as such. Neither has been offsetting its chronic export surplus by foreign lending and investment. This fact makes for a *permanent* imbalance which threatens all attempts at currency stabilization.

In 1958 the Bonn government began to react to long-continued pressure, especially from the underdeveloped countries. The chronic West German export surplus rose in the first six months of 1958 to $620 million. In August the German government diverted $100 million from domestic reconstruction to financing the export of capital goods to underdeveloped countries, allowing them eight years in which to repay. The Bonn government also joined in making international loans to India and Turkey. At the same time, a serious effort was made to increase German imports.

The United States, however, has remained very far from fulfilling its function as the world's largest creditor and exporter. It still permits only a trickle of competitive foreign goods to enter its great mass market and barely maintains its relatively low level of foreign investment. The inadequacy of American import of goods and export of capital for constructive purposes has been partially obscured by the fact that military aid, defense-support grants, and the expenditures of over 1,500,000 Americans stationed abroad have annually taken a substantial amount of dollars out of the country. Were this not the case, the world-wide shortage of dollars would have become even more of an impediment to trade and economic development.

The chief reason for the so-called "dollar gap" is quite simply that the United States has unintentionally been sabotaging the workings of that free-market economy which Americans so vehemently defend in theory. By failing either to increase its imports or to get rid of the hot money created by a chronic export surplus—by failing to fulfill the proper functions of a creditor nation—the United States is, in fact, stimulating the increase of precisely that kind of government interference in international trade which it deplores.

(c) Other Elements of Internal Weakness

There are other elements of internal weakness in the economic life of the West about which it is difficult to generalize, because their importance varies widely in the different national environments within the Western community.

Broadly speaking, the Western economy as a whole suffers from chronic, creeping inflation paradoxically accompanied by an apparent inability to achieve stable prosperity without a continual expansion of production in excess of effective consumer demand. Above all, the Western economy suffers from dependence upon military expenditures as a stimulus to economic activity; thus it has acquired a dangerous vested interest in *not* making peace.

Since these characteristics are most pronounced in the economically most important member of the Western community, it will be more useful to defer a more specific discussion to a later chapter dealing with the economy of the United States.

It should be emphasized here, however, that in a world in which a major war means extinction the Western economy is still geared to the preparation for precisely such a war. It has not yet adjusted itself to the assumptions of peace upon which all hope of survival must be predicated.

2. THE WEST AND THE UNCOMMITTED PEOPLES

The relationship of the Western community to the uncommitted peoples is, in the first instance, political and psychological rather than economic.

Here the outstanding weakness of the West is that it has no common policy. The historical reason for this is self-evident.

Great Britain, France, Belgium, and the Netherlands are the last of the great colonial powers. Spain and Portugal long ago lost most of their once great empires. Two late-comers, Germany and Italy, forfeited their overseas possessions as the result of lost wars—Germany after World War I, and Italy after World War II. The United States, itself once a colonial dependency, acquired its only colonial possessions in a short-lived fit of imperialism at the turn of the century and freed them prior to the onset of the anti-colonial revolution.

The uncommitted peoples of Asia and Africa are, for the most part, peoples formerly belonging to the empires or spheres of influence of Great Britain, France, and the Netherlands. These three countries have pursued widely divergent policies both in the administration of their empires and with respect to their recent partial liquidation. Britain has retreated more gracefully than the Netherlands; the Netherlands has retreated with somewhat better grace than France. Britain—except in the Middle East—has left behind a minimum of resentment; France has left a maximum.

The United States, by nature ideally fitted to act as a mediator between the stubborn retentiveness of the colonial powers and the hyperfervid haste of the formerly dependent peoples in seeking independence, has failed to fulfill this role. It has wavered uncertainly between support and obstruction of the colonial revolution. Its policy in Asia and the Middle East has been shaped more by strategic considerations and concern for allies and bases than by political reflection. On balance, the United States has identified itself more with the colonial powers than with the emerging peoples.

American prestige and influence have sustained further damage among the uncommitted peoples from the fact that, among all the Western nations, the United States alone was in a position to be able to extend economic assistance on a large scale. The Point Four program held out the promise of such aid, but the promise remained unfulfilled. American aid flowed on a relatively small scale to Asia and Africa, and then primarily to those of the emerging peoples who were willing to give up their non-alignment in the communist-anti-communist power struggle.

Thus the Western community has appeared to the uncommitted peoples as dominated by an unsympathetic and bellicose American leader who aroused new resentment instead of mitigating the old resentments which had grown out of colonial rule. It is a striking fact that, in Southeast Asia, Britain is more popular than the United States.

The first and most obvious conclusion to be drawn from past experience is that the efforts of the Western nations should be co-ordinated in a common policy toward the uncommitted peoples.

Leaving aside for the moment the question of *what* common policy, it would seem desirable that no single Western nation, least of all the United States, should appear as the dominant factor in co-ordinated Western action.

A further conclusion might be that it would be wise to enlist in the formulation and execution of Western policy nations, such as Germany and the Scandinavian countries, which are not associated with the idea of colonialism. In addition, it might be helpful to draw in some of the Latin-American countries, such as Mexico and Uruguay, which have made considerable political and economic progress but still share many of the problems and aspirations of the emerging peoples of Asia and Africa.

As to *what* common policy the West should adopt, the most important thing to be said is that it be a policy shaped in consultation with the peoples whose economic development it is intended to assist. This end could probably best be accomplished by some form of joint regional organization including both the contributing nations and those requiring assistance.

49

Various proposals for multilateral action have been put forward in the past, only to fall afoul of the American government's preference for bilateral agreements.

The Afro-Asian bloc of newly independent nations has long urged the creation of a "Special United Nations Fund for Economic Development" (SUNFED). This proposal failed to enlist the support of the United States and other industrialized member nations.

Various students of Middle Eastern affairs, among them the writer, have advocated the creation of a Middle East Development Authority—a proposal endorsed in the United States Senate by Hubert H. Humphrey of Minnesota. The Latin-American nations have urged the setting up of an Inter-American Bank. Both of these regional proposals were turned down by the Eisenhower administration until August 13, 1958, when, as we shall see presently, it suddenly reversed its position.

Early in 1957 the writer put forward a plan for the creation of a United Nations Development Authority with regional subsidiaries in each of the six major underdeveloped areas. A feature of this plan was that it provided for specific machinery by which fair representation on the Authority would be given both to the contributing industrialized nations and to the underdeveloped nations seeking assistance. The proposal was endorsed by the American Association for the United Nations and by the Commission to Study the Organization of Peace but was not seriously considered by the American government.[2]

Later in 1957, United States Senator A. S. Mike Monroney of Oklahoma sponsored a proposal to create an International Development Association, linked to the International Bank for Reconstruction and Development (The World Bank). This proposal, at first rejected by the Eisenhower administration, finally received its qualified approval.[3]

As we shall see presently, Vice-President Nixon's experience

[2]*Proposal for a United Nations Development Authority*, Current Affairs Press, 1957. *Strengthening the United Nations* (The Commission's 1957 Report), Harper, 1957.

[3]See President Eisenhower's letter to Secretary of the Treasury Anderson in the New York *Times* of August 26, 1958.

in Latin America and the Middle East crisis of 1958 had the effect of unfreezing to some extent at least the American government's rigid position against regionalizing or internationalizing aid to world economic development.

It is true that until some of the existing tensions between the West and the communist orbit are relaxed, it may not be possible to channel economic aid to the underdeveloped areas through the United Nations, although the writer believes that the Western nations should sponsor such a proposal and put it squarely up to the Kremlin. For the time being, the Monroney plan for a World Bank subsidiary may be more feasible than the author's more far-reaching proposal, but it must be borne in mind that the World Bank is a purely Western institution and that the ultimate aim should be to lift aid to economic development altogether out of the framework of the cold war. Moreover, the ultimate aim should be to strengthen the United Nations rather than to create more outside organizations which, no matter how useful, may tend to deprive the world organization of some of its proper functions.

An extremely important by-product of the internationalization of economic aid—whether through a United Nations Development Authority, a World Bank subsidiary, or regional institutions—would be the wider use of technicians and advisers not only from every part of the Western community but from non-Western nations such as Japan. This would avoid an over-heavy influx of personnel from any one country, particularly from the United States.

In addition to taking care of the distribution of technical and capital assistance, whatever regional or supra-national agency or agencies may be created should be charged with the promotion of international trade both among the underdeveloped peoples and between them and the industrialized countries.

The stabilization of the world prices of the major primary products is central to this problem.

Most of the underdeveloped countries depend upon the export of foodstuffs or raw materials. Some depend upon a single crop, as for instance Brazil upon coffee, Cuba upon sugar,

51

Ghana upon cocoa, or Egypt upon cotton. Others depend upon minerals or other industrial raw materials, as for instance Bolivia upon tin, Chile upon copper, Ceylon upon rubber and tea, Malaya upon rubber and tin, and so on. Iran, Iraq, Saudi Arabia, and the Persian Gulf sheikdoms depend upon oil; so does Venezuela.

The industrialized nations of the West provide the market for most of these foodstuffs and raw materials, the United States being by far the heaviest importer.

The trouble is that with the exception of monopolistically controlled oil—which is a separate and distinct matter to be discussed presently—the industrialized nations of the West do not provide a *steady* market. The fluctuations in their demand cause alternating sharp rises and falls in world prices. This unstabilizes the economies of the primary producing countries. War, the threat of war, or a business boom creates a rising demand, rising prices and prosperity; a relaxation of tensions or a business recession in the West causes a falling demand, falling prices, and depression. It has been estimated that the 1957-58 recession in the United States cost the raw-material-producing countries something like five billion dollars—considerably more than the entire American economic-aid program for the same period.

It is readily apparent that it is almost impossible to plan a development program for a country exposed to these hazards. It must be equally apparent that Western failure to respond to the repeated pleas of raw-material producers for some sort of price stabilization arouses deep resentment. This resentment is magnified by the fact that where the West has an interest as the producer of a foodstuff or a primary material—for example, in wheat and, above all, in oil—it has devised price-stabilization schemes which are quite effective.

The objections to commodity price stabilization schemes are: (1) that they are complicated and difficult to operate, unless, as in the case of oil, there is a producer's monopoly, and (2) that they run counter to the theory of the free market. The first objection is valid but not conclusive, as evidenced by the existing wheat and sugar agreements. The second objection, which comes chiefly from the United States, is on an intellectual par with recurring proposals to limit American economic aid to countries where there is a "free capitalist economy."

A foreign country dependent upon raw-material export may be pardoned for thinking that this sort of economic religiosity comes strangely from a nation whose government makes a practice of protecting its own agriculture by price supports and its industry by tariffs. Similarly, an Indian or a Burmese might be pardoned for inquiring just how it is possible to organize a captalist economy in a country where there is little or no private capital.

Commodity price stabilization is a *must*, if the West wishes to develop constructive economic relations with the under-developed nations. It is even more important than direct assistance toward economic development, for, without it, economic assistance will remain largely ineffective.

Continued failure to recognize and act upon this imperative need will constitute a serious threat to intra-Western economic health as well as to the relationships of the highly industrialized Western nations with Latin America and with the uncommitted third of the world's peoples.

The situation as to oil is quite different.

Eight giant oil companies—five of them American—control the non-communist world's supply of oil, maintaining administered prices which have nothing to do with supply and demand and which yield exorbitant profits. The practices of the five American companies have, since 1952, been the object of desultory action by the Anti-Trust Division of the United States Department of Justice. The charges against the companies cover in great detail the methods and devices by which the defendants are alleged to "monopolize trade and commerce in petroleum and petroleum products between the United States and foreign nations."

In essence, these charges amount to this: that the oil companies extract oil from the Middle East, which contains 90 per cent of the known reserves of the non-communist world, at a cost of 20 to 30 cents a barrel and sell it at a collusive price varying over a period of recent years from $1.75 to $2.16 per barrel, f.o.b. the Persian Gulf.

The resulting profit has, as a rule, been split on a fifty-fifty basis with the government of the country in which the oil is produced. This royalty has been charged off as an income tax levied by the foreign governments, thus drastically reducing the income tax due to the United States government. In addition, the international companies profit by 27 per cent depletion allowance, written into the American tax law to encourage domestic oil exploration, although the cost of exploration in the Middle East is only a small fraction of what it is in the United States. From 1933 to 1955 the largest of the American companies operating in the Middle East—the Arabian-American Oil Company—paid no income tax whatever to the American government. In 1956 it paid $282,000 on profits estimated at $200 million, after paying a like amount to the King of Saudi Arabia.

There is far more at stake here than a possible infringement of the anti-trust laws. There is involved not only an abuse of the American taxpayer but a flagrant abuse of the consumer of petroleum products throughout the non-communist world.

The fact that the countries of Western Europe, Africa, Southeast Asia, and Latin America must pay something like $2.00 a barrel for oil which comes out of the Middle East at a cost of something like 20 cents impairs their dollar reserves, retards their development, and increases their need for economic assistance. This creates an additional burden upon the industrialized nations which desire to promote world economic development.

Moreover, the oil combine clearly violates the principle of equal access for all nations at reasonable prices to the world's raw materials—a principle to which the Western nations solemnly pledged themselves in the so-called United Nations Declaration of January 1942.[4]

[4]The term "United Nations" was at that time used to denote the anti-Axis coalition. The United Nations organization did not, of course, then exist. The declaration referred to was a reaffirmation by the major members of the wartime coalition of the principles enunciated by President Roosevelt and Prime Minister Churchill in the Atlantic Charter of August 1941.

Since the United States is both the chief consumer of raw materials and the major potential source of capital for world economic development, these questions will be examined further in connection with American foreign economic policy (Chapter Five).

3. WESTERN ECONOMIC RELATIONS WITH THE COMMUNIST ORBIT

For the past decade Western economic policy with respect to the Soviet bloc—especially United States policy—has been to restrict trade almost as completely as it has been customary in times of war to restrict trade with an enemy.

The American lead has not always been followed by other members of the Western community, some of whom have felt that the embargo was unwise while others have insisted upon trading with the communist countries out of alleged necessity. On the whole, the reluctance to follow the American lead has been increasing; and recently there have been indications that even the United States is moving toward a thinning out of the embargo.

The origin of the policy of trade restriction was, of course, the desire to deprive the communist dictatorships of war-making potential. Hence the prohibition upon the export to the Soviet bloc of a long list of strategic materials. At first this policy was intimately related to the careful guarding of secrets relating to the manufacture of atomic weapons. Once Russia had these weapons in sufficient quantity to destroy the West, the whole policy lost much of its original rationale.

Additionally, the economic iron curtain was perforated by the defection of Yugoslavia and the semi-defection of Poland, raising the question whether aid and trade should be permitted to flow to countries which were communist but independent or semi-independent of Soviet control.

During the period in which the restrictive policy was, for one reason or another, being slowly diluted, the most important questions concerning that policy were scarcely raised and debated, except perhaps in the secret conference rooms of some of the Western foreign offices. These questions might be formulated thus:

Does the economic embargo actually hurt the communist dictatorships, or does it perhaps help them? If it hurts them, does it hurt them more than it hurts the nations of the West? Does the policy reduce the danger of war, or does it increase tensions and the likelihood of war?

From what we know, self-sufficiency lies at the core of communist economic policy—not *national* self-sufficiency, which is unattainable in the modern world, but *bloc* self-sufficiency, which, given the size and diversified resources of the Sino-Soviet orbit, is probably not an unattainable objective. We know that in every vital sphere of production the dictatorships have made great efforts to become self-sufficient, and that the central Soviet planning machinery has endeavored to integrate the national economies of the bloc into one over-all economic machine. We do not know to what extent this central planning includes China, but we do know that each of the Soviet satellites has been assigned its special tasks—tasks for which it is best fitted in the interests of bloc self-sufficiency. We are also reasonably sure that, to the extent that China operates independently, it too is seeking self-sufficiency.

Given these facts, or these assumptions, does the Western embargo help or hinder the development of Sino-Soviet self-sufficiency?

It has long been the opinion of this observer that, on the whole, the Western policy of restriction has tended to further rather than retard the achievement of communist aims.

If, for example, the West had been willing to supply the Soviet Union and China with machine tools, it seems at least doubtful whether so much of the communist effort would have gone into building their own machine-tool industry. The same thing applies to finished industrial machines. Had there been no embargo, Soviet and Chinese development might have proceeded along somewhat different lines, with light industry receiving more attention, as it has in other recently industrialized countries which could draw upon the basic heavy industries of the West. In any case, the communist countries would have tended to acquire a self-interest in trading with the West for the sake of accelerating their industrialization, and the West would have enjoyed a profitable business involving not only the initial sales but the supplying of spare parts and replacements. This is precisely the sort of business which German heavy industry has been markedly successful in building up with Latin America. Leaving aside political considerations, such a relationship would, in fact, have been the logical sequel to Lend-Lease.

It may be held that the political cleavages which developed after World War II made such a development impossible. This observer would be inclined to reply that a non-restrictive Western policy—except for actual military equipment—might have gone far toward easing the tensions resulting from those cleavages. Admittedly, this is conjecture, but the effect of the restrictive policy upon the West is evident beyond conjecture.

The economic blockade has deprived the West European countries of markets which they badly needed, especially in view of the fact that the American market was largely unavailable to them. It has caused sharp differences between the United States and Britain and between the United States and Canada, where the American restrictive policy was enforced upon Canadian subsidiaries of American concerns. It has damaged United States relations with Japan, which has been prevented by American pressure from seeking business in its traditional trading area.

The restrictive policy has not only created dissension within the Western world but has also tended to strengthen the Sino-Soviet alliance by making China utterly dependent upon the Soviet Union for machine tools and other essentials for industrialization, including the services of Soviet technicians and engineers.

All in all, whatever may have been the strategic justification for the restrictive policy in the past, it is difficult to see how its discontinuance could now make the communists any more of a military threat than they already are.

On the other hand, it seems to this observer well worth considering whether a resumption of something like normal trade

relations might not contribute substantially to an easing of
tensions which, in turn, would contribute toward diminishing
the likelihood of war.

We come now to the question of the Western attitude toward
communist competition in economic aid and trade with the
non-communist nations of Asia, Africa, and Latin America.

Western leadership has belatedly become concerned over
such competition because of the somewhat spectacular political
gains scored by the communists in certain sensitive areas. It is
important to see this threat in terms of the future rather than
solely in terms of the present—not to overestimate the present
Sino-Soviet capabilities nor to underestimate their possible development.

Above all, it is important for the West not to distort its economic policies through a panicky effort to meet communist
competition on its own terms.

As of the present, the Sino-Soviet bloc does not begin to com-
pare with the Western community either as a market for the
primary producers or as a potential supplier of the needs of the
underdeveloped countries. The Soviet bloc's imports from non-
communist Asia, Africa, and Latin America amounted in 1956
to only about 3 per cent of world imports. Soviet exports are
strictly limited by the pressing demands of the rapidly growing
Soviet economy and by the urgent needs of China. The export
of capital is limited by the same factors; an analysis of the
highly publicized "foreign loans" made by the Soviet Union
shows that most of them consist of barter agreements or credits
for the purchase of Soviet goods.

Soviet competition appears formidable because, in spite of
limited resources, communist leadership has exercised remarkable political skill in selecting its points of intervention. In
Egypt and Syria, the sale of arms, the purchase of cotton, and
a series of trade agreements, plus the shipment of medical supplies refused to Egypt by the United States, enabled the Kremlin to establish a political bridgehead in an area which Russia
had long vainly sought to penetrate. In Ceylon, Burma, and
the Sudan, the communists acquired a considerable amount of

good will through timely purchases of burdensome stocks of primary commodities. India is being wooed by the erection of a steel mill and the demonstration of Soviet engineering skill. Afghanistan has had the streets of its capital paved and has received other not large but psychologically important benefits.

Most of these opportunities were created by Western ineptitude or neglect. The penetration of Egypt and Syria was made possible by a long series of Western diplomatic blunders. The rearming of Pakistan alienated both India and Afghanistan, leaving them susceptible to communist blandishments. When Burma was surfeited with rice and Ceylon with rubber, the Western nations saw no need to help them out of their difficulties.

The Achilles' heel of the crafty communist economic policy—its strictly political motivation—has been kept from exposure by the much more overt political conditions attached to Western aid. Where communist aid is given in such a way that the recipient can only suspect political motives, Western aid is either openly conditioned upon outright alliance against the communist bloc or given with the unconcealed hope of wooing the uncommitted nations out of their non-alignment. When aid from both sides is suspect, the inevitable result is that the seekers of aid play off one side against the other.

Rather than compete with the communists at their own game, it seems evident that the West would profit by divorcing its economic policy toward the uncommitted peoples from the cold war altogether. Instead of rushing in to forestall the acceptance of communist assistance in economic development, the West might be wiser to welcome such assistance, saying to a country like India: "If the Russians will build you a steel mill, so much the better; in that case we can use our resources to build you an oil refinery."

At the present time, communist competition in aiding the economic development of the uncommitted peoples is serious only because of the defects of Western policy; these can be summarized as niggardliness and obsession with the cold war.

The real danger lies in the future. Soviet production is growing roughly twice as fast as that of the United States. China is already a substantial exporter of textiles, cement, sewing machines, typewriters, ceramics, and other low-priced consumer goods. The Chinese are underselling the Japanese in Indonesia and undercutting British and Indian trade in Malaya and Singapore. At the present rates of growth, the time is not far distant when Sino-Soviet capabilities for aid and trade will catch up to the capabilities of the West.

This raises two problems:

Can Western economic growth be sufficiently accelerated to preserve its lead? And can the West, during the next few years, develop economic relationships with the underdeveloped countries which will prove lasting, no matter what the communist challenge, because they rest upon mutual trust and mutually happy experience in co-operative effort?

The answer to the second question has already been indicated: The West can develop such relationships if it puts its own house in order, integrates Latin America in the Western community, dissociates its economic relationships with the uncommitted peoples from the cold war, and internationalizes its assistance to their development.

The economy of the United States is probably the key factor in determining whether the growth of the Western economy can be sufficiently accelerated to keep its productivity ahead of that of the communist orbit. This will be briefly examined in the next chapter.

It should be emphasized here, however, that what might be called "the crisis of capitalism" does not arise from the communist challenge but from the inner defects in the Western economic structure and the defects of Western policy, some of which have been touched upon in this chapter.

The Western economic structure does not represent "capitalism" in the Marxist meaning of that term. Nor does it for that reason contain the seeds of its own *inevitable* destruction. The Western economic structure does contain a number of *curable* weaknesses which, if left uncured, may encompass its destruction.

The communist challenge has merely moved up the deadline for remedial action.

CHAPTER FOUR

Soft Spots in the American Economy

I

The economy of the United States is critically important to the
Western economic system not merely because of its size and
weight and because of its impact upon other national economies
but for another reason; namely, that in the United States
"capitalism" has successfully developed to a point where its
acquisitive dynamic is approaching exhaustion.

In no other country of the world has a free-enterprise system,
regulated with the minimum of government interference so as
to serve the general welfare, achieved such success. In no other
country has the broad mass of the population attained such a
high level of income, such a profusion of possessions, or such
a wide choice of amenities and luxuries. In no other country
have the enclaves of poverty been so rapidly reduced. In no
other country is work easier or pay higher.

And yet . . .

American "capitalism" faces a crisis because its very success
is gradually emasculating the incentives which have hitherto
propelled it to such heights. Contrary to the belief widely held
by other peoples that Americans care only about money and
physical possessions, the desire to get rich, to own a large house
or estate, and to indulge in what Veblen called "conspicuous
consumption" no longer dominates the majority of Americans.
To most American boys getting out of school or college the ideal

61

sought is a secure job yielding an income of perhaps $15,000—enough to support a wife and three or four children in a suburban house with a two-car garage costing $35,000 or $40,000 to be paid for over a period of years. This dream house will, of course, be equipped with all the standard appliances, including television and perhaps a hi-fi radio—all bought on the installment plan. The young American has almost ceased to want more than his fellow American; he wants "what everybody else has"—no more and no less.

Similarly, in an economy characterized by huge corporate enterprises, the drive for personal power has become attenuated. With few exceptions, Americans no longer dream of personal empires and, in any case, the income tax has made such dreams unrealistic, except for oil magnates, who enjoy special privilege in the form of depletion allowance.

John Kenneth Galbraith, professor of economics at Harvard University, has brilliantly pointed out[1] that, in the American economy of today, goods are produced less and less because people want them and more and more because their production provides steady employment. The reason advertisers so frantically press their products upon the consumer is that so much of the American effort goes into producing a demand for the "unnecessary goods which provide highly necessary jobs." Galbraith rightly cocks a quizzical eyebrow at this state of affairs and raises the question whether Americans have not failed to recognize that the disappearance of mass poverty inevitably reduces the mass demand for additional possessions.

If Professor Galbraith is right—and this writer happens to think that in this respect he is—then his observation constitutes a warning which should be heeded not only by Americans but by any and all of the world's peoples who regard the United States as the model of a successful free-enterprise economy. For what Galbraith tells us amounts to this:

A free-enterprise economy, successfully regulated in the public interest so as to produce a wide distribution of prosperity, is very likely to slow down and eventually come to a halt unless

[1] J. K. Galbraith, *The Affluent Society*, Houghton Mifflin, 1958.

wholly new private incentives are developed and new public policies are adopted.

To say this is not to say that a capitalist economy should not be regulated in the public interest. On the contrary, it remains true that capitalism, if not harnessed to the greatest good of the greatest number, either turns into some form of fascism or else is superseded by some form of socialism.

But, paradoxically, the more capitalism becomes "people's capitalism"—to use a currently popular phrase—the more it tends to run out of gas. Its very success in supplying what people want leaves it with fewer and fewer wants to fulfill.

One may question some of Professor Galbraith's further conclusions, but this quite novel postulate may well mark a milestone in the progress of economic thought, equal in importance to the contributions of J. Maynard Keynes (later Lord Keynes) a generation ago. In fact, Galbraith seems to this student of economics to have cut through to the central problem of an economy of abundance very much as Keynes put his finger on the central problem of an economy of scarcity.

II

In a pamphlet[2] published in mid-1956 warning, among other things, of the imminence of a serious economic setback in the then booming American economy, this observer set forth three dangerous weaknesses in the American economic structure which now appear in a new light by reason of Galbraith's postulate. The three points emphasized were:

1. The overstimulation of consumer demand by advertising and other sales pressures, together with the overexpansion of consumer credit.

2. The unhealthy contrast between private extravagance and public parsimony, except for military spending.

3. The dangerous dependence of the American economy upon military expenditures—in other words, upon a continuation of the cold war.

It was pointed out that the excessive consumer borrowing

[2]*Danger and Opportunity*, Current Affairs Press, 1956.

might easily turn any minor business recession into a serious downward spiral, causing unemployment on a large scale, a general loss of confidence, and, quite likely, a damaging effect upon the precariously balanced economies of other nations. Prolonged distress in the farm sector of the economy had, at this time, already affected factory employment. While a few labor leaders had taken alarm, labor's action on the whole had been confined to securing additional wage increases while the going was still good. It was pointed out that employers were consistently raising prices to the consumer to a greater extent than seemed warranted by the wage increases granted.

It appeared to this observer that businessmen were paying insufficient attention to the danger signals, proceeding to enlarge their plants in the belief that, at worst, a minor setback might occur, after which the demands of a rising population would be greater than ever. This attitude of the business community clearly rested upon the assumption that continued government spending for military hardware at the rate of about thirty-five billion dollars a year would provide a guarantee against a major depression. At the same time, the government was cutting down military expenditures on the theory of "more bang for a buck," without even considering any increase in its domestic programs.

These facts seemed to this observer to warrant alarm.

Subsequent events have justified the warning, but Galbraith's deeper insights illuminate the superficiality of the writer's 1956 analysis. This observer could merely point out *what* was happening. The Galbraith postulate offers an explanation of *why* it happened and is likely to happen again.

The 1957–58 recession has, for the time being, corrected some of the factors which caused it. Consumer borrowing has declined; inventories have been reduced; plant expansion has slowed down. The cold war has taken a turn for the worse and military spending is again on the increase.

But basically nothing has changed. Prices are still rising faster than wages and incomes. It is still assumed that, when the trouble is over, people will once more be glad to buy whatever the manufacturers make and the advertising agencies tell them they cannot live without.

Perhaps so, for a few years. But, if Galbraith is right, the handwriting is on the wall. At some time in the not-far-distant future people are going to stop creating necessary jobs by buying unnecessary things. At some point, surfeit will defeat sales pressure.

The well-known sociologist, David Riesman, confirms Galbraith's postulate from a study of human behavior rather than from the point of view of an economist.[3] Riesman, too, comes to the conclusion that in the American society the old incentives are wearing out and that new incentives are needed. The symbols of social status are changing along with the changing aims and ambitions of American men and women.

III

Quite apart from the long-range view of the American economy, there are certain other factors which tend to increase consumer resistance and thus to invalidate the assumption that there is no limit to what people can be induced to buy. The decline in the *quality* of goods offered is certainly one such factor. The unrelenting insistence of advertising with its endless repetition may be another. But the most important deterrent to consumer buying at the present time is without doubt the so-called inflation, which causes prices of goods to rise faster than wages and spendable consumer income.

Actually this phenomenon is not "inflation" in the classical sense at all. Prices in the United States are not at present rising because the demand for goods exceeds the supply, as it did during and immediately after World War II. Nor are prices rising, as they did in the early days of the New Deal, primarily because an artificial increase in the supply of money and credit was depreciating the purchasing power of the dollar.

The chief reason for "inflation in the midst of a depression"— the phenomenon which has puzzled so many business analysts—

[3]David Riesman, "Abundance for What?" an article in the March 1958 issue of *The Progressive*.

is that prices in the United States are no longer determined primarily by demand and supply but by the collusive fixing of prices by big industry and big labor. The price rise during the 1957–58 recession has been a manipulated price rise, not a natural phenomenon.

The report of the Senate Subcommittee on Anti-Trust and Monopoly, of which Senator Estes Kefauver of Tennessee is the chairman, brought out some illuminating facts in this regard. Taking the steel industry as an example, the report showed that, while the wage adjustment of July 1957 added between $2.50 and $3.00 to the cost of producing a ton of steel, the steel companies immediately added $6.00 to the price, and this in spite of the fact that a drop in the cost of steel scrap, an important element in steel-making, had probably more than offset the cost of the wage increase. The fact that prices have been raised far above the increase in costs is shown by the following tabulation of the net profit (after taxes) per ton of steel shipped by the United States Steel Corporaton.

1952	$ 6.80
1953	8.85
1954	9.15
1955	14.51
1956	14.56
1957	17.91

Inasmuch as steel production was declining in 1956–57, the only possible explanation for the company's increased profits is that prices were raised higher than increased costs.

In a competitive industry, such price manipulation would be impossible. It is possible in the steel industry because when the United States Steel Corporation raises its price the other producers raise their prices to the same level.[4]

The Senate subcommittee found that much the same condi-

[4] In July 1958, perhaps as a result of the Kefauver investigation, a smaller steel company was permitted to make the initial move in raising prices "to meet the wage increase." Within twenty-four hours the entire industry followed suit. The price rise amounted to about $4.50 per ton of steel, a figure probably considerably in excess of the cost per ton of the the wage increase but not as flagrantly so as in the preceding year.

tions prevailed in the automobile industry, the oil industry, and others which it examined.

The polite term for this monopolistic price fixing was invented by the economist, Gardiner C. Means, who described prices not set by the workings of supply and demand as "administered prices." Dr. Means and many other experts believe that administered prices are to a degree inevitable in a modern industrial economy. The Senate subcommittee did not find that administered prices were objectionable *per se*. The subcommittee was concerned with *how* the prices were administered and especially with why they should be administered upward even at a time when an industry was working at something like half its capacity. It was concerned with the fact that to all intents and purposes such practices eliminated the natural correctives in time of recession.

Dr. Ludwig Erhard, Vice-Chancellor and Economics Minister of the German Federal Republic, who is generally credited with being the chief architect of West Germany's phenomenal resurgence, made this interesting comment in June 1958 after a visit to the United States.[5]

> The one alarming symptom I have observed in the American economy is the decline in production coinciding with a rise in prices. Any real entrepreneurial activity implies the risk of loss as well as the chance of profit. It is therefore against the spirit of free enterprise to raise prices in an attempt to maintain profits at a certain standard, regardless of production and sales . . . It is necessary in a free economy to keep prices flexible so that they will respond to market fluctuations.

Senator Kefauver believes that there are three ways in which the abuse of administered prices might be corrected: "By restraint on the part of the producers, by some form of government control, or by restoring the administered-price industries to conditions approaching those of true competition." He remarks that "moderation seems to have become a forgotten virtue

[5]*Life* magazine, June 9, 1958.

among the ranks of our large corporations." He thinks, however, that the pressure of an aroused public opinon might restore some of this lost virtue and prefers the attempt to arouse public opinion to government intervention, which he thinks should be regarded as a last resort. As to the anti-trust approach, Senator Kefauver says:

> Conceptually, anti-trust is the antithesis of direct price regulation in that it would destroy monopoly rather than accept its existence and try to control it. In that sense, it is the more far-reaching approach.

But the senator goes on to say that the principal argument against the anti-trust approach is that it is widely held to run counter to the requirements of efficiency and innovation.[6]

The writer is inclined to agree with Senator Kefauver that the most promising approach is to arouse public opinion—to make people understand and protest against the profiteering, monopolistic practices which cause the cost of living to mount year after year, irrespective of boom or depression.

The question is: *how* to arouse public opinion?

A report like that of the Senate subcommittee receives scant attention in the mass media of communication.

"The failure of the mass media in the public opinion area is due to their growing emphasis on entertainment rather than information," says Mr. Lester Markel, one of the leading American newspaper editors.[7] He continues: "If the mass media do not have a full sense of public responsibility, what basic reason is there for their existence and for their privileges?"

Mr. Markel raises a question which affects every aspect of domestic and foreign policy, but he does not suggest how to persuade the managers of the mass media to think more of their responsibilities and—like the big industrialists—to think a little less of their profits.

The mass media are Big Business; like industry, they live off the mass market for consumer goods and the mass appetite

[6]Estes Kefauver, "Manipulated Price Rise," *The Nation*, June 28, 1958.

[7]Lester Markel in the *Sunday New York Times Magazine* of July 13, 1958.

for entertainment. The American people apparently would rather be drenched in advertising, for which they pay in higher prices of consumer goods, than pay the full cost of their entertainment and of such information as they are given by the mass media. (How many people would buy the daily *New York Times* if they had to pay twenty-five cents a copy or whatever it costs to produce it?) Can the mass media change the American people? Or must the people, learning through hard experience, influence the media?

The latter is more likely to be the case.

IV

By far the most serious weakness in the American economy is its dependence upon military expenditures. It is no exaggeration to say that, if a disarmament agreement were to be reached on, let us say, next Monday, the American economy would go into a tailspin on Tuesday. By the time plans were made to meet this emergency, the United States would find itself paralyzed by a major depression.

This state of affairs is as dangerous as it is unnecessary.

It is dangerous not only in itself but because it creates a serious obstacle to making peace. It creates an atmosphere in which people are compelled to associate disarmament with the loss of jobs and the loss of profits, instead of thinking of it as a boon. A barber in the little town of Brunswick, Maine, told the writer: "If we get disarmament and they take away the Naval Air Station, my business will be cooked." The growing vested interest in having the cold war continue is a formidable inpediment to ending it.

It is utterly unnecessary for this condition to exist. Here we come up against the curious discrepancy between the American attitudes toward private and public expenditures. The American family budget is chronically unbalanced. As individuals, Americans habitually spend more than they earn by borrowing against their future earning power. However, when it comes to public expenditure, Americans are not only mesmerized by the fetish of a balanced budget but wholly misled as to their nation's capabilities within the limits of maintaining a balanced budget. Because the government is spending $35 billion to $40 billion a year on unproductive armaments, the ordinary citizen is led to believe that the government cannot afford to make even the most necessary productive expenditures without either irresponsibly increasing the national debt or imposing additional taxes.

This is arrant nonsense. Wisely planned public expenditures combined with proper incentives to private investment would result only in a *larger* budget, not an *unbalanced* budget; the resulting increased growth in the economy would produce greater revenues at current rates of taxation and would eventually result in a reduction of taxes. The accent here is on *wisely planned* public expenditures combined with incentives to private activity. Public spending alone will not do the job. It depends upon how and for what public money is spent.

In the preceding chapter mention was made of the fact that the Soviet economy is growing at about double the annual growth rate of the United States. This is only in part because the Soviet Union is able to achieve a remarkably rapid growth through forced savings and deprivation of the consumer. It is also due to the fact that the growth of the American economy has actually been slowing down.

We are badly misled by statistics which show that the gross national product is each year higher than in the year before. The truth of the matter is that the United States needs an overall annual economic expansion of about 4.5 per cent to keep pace with the growing labor force and the displacement of labor through technological progress. *If the United States economy shows less than an annual growth of about 4.5 per cent it is actually not growing at all but going backward.*

Leon H. Keyserling, president of the Conference on Economic Progress, estimates that, whereas the 4.5 per cent growth rate had been exceeded from 1947 to 1953 (partly owing to the stimulus of the Korean War), it slowed down during 1953–57 from a little better than 2.5 per cent to 2 per cent and to a rate of less than 1 per cent in the last quarter of 1957. Keyserling estimates that from 1953 to 1957 the United States lost "more than $78 billion worth of potential production and about 8.5 million man years of potential job opportunity through departures from full employment."[8]

One need not accept these estimates as 100 per cent correct to see that during the past five years the United States has suffered a gigantic shortfall in possible and badly needed economic growth. In part, this deficit was caused by the policies of Big Business discussed in the preceding section, policies which reduced consumer purchasing power and plowed excessive profits into plant investment. In even larger measure the shortfall was caused by the economic policies of the government. Artificially tight money and fiscal "conservatism" encouraged Big Business to do the wrong things, at the same time curtailing the building of schools, new housing, and resource development.

A high point of regressive government policy was reached on January 9, 1958, when, under the impact of the Soviet sputniks, President Eisenhower announced in his State of the Union message that increased military expenditures would be required but that they would be largely offset by "savings" in "certain domestic programs." In other words, the cost of catching up to the Russians in missile development was to be offset in large part by reducing expenditures for education, health, and other social services. This meant that, instead of being borne by the people as a whole, the additional military expenditures were to be borne chiefly by the children, the aged, the sick, and those elements of the population least able to look after themselves. Fortunately Congress did not follow this recommendation. (The January 1959 Budget Message followed the same pattern.)

For the United States to stop going backward—not to mention catching up to the Soviet rate of growth—at least these requirements must be fulfilled:

Big Business must mend its ways and stop combining with Big Labor to fleece the consumer. Labor leadership, remembering that workers are consumers, must stop reaching for wage increases not warranted by increased productivity and better

[8]Leon Keyserling, "The Economy in 1958," in the *New Republic* of January 13, 1958.

workmanship. Government must stop being penny-wise and pound-foolish, reversing its regressive policies and setting out in earnest to fulfill the requirements of the Full Employment Act passed by the Congress in 1946.

This almost forgotten piece of legislation requires the President of the United States each year to present to Congress an estimate of the levels of production and employment required for the nation's welfare, along with recommendations for public and private action toward the achievement of these goals.

The statutory basis for the needed action exists. What has been lacking during the past five years is the will to carry out the law's requirements.

The kind of "conservatism" which has governed public policy under the Eisenhower administration does not conserve the nation's strength. It jeopardizes the nation's security. It permits the nation's assets to waste away, its land to be eroded and washed into the sea, its resources to be developed more for private profit than for public good, and its children's future to be irreparably impaired. This is not conservatism. It is irresponsible waste, dictated by self-interest pressure groups and rationalized by the bookkeeping rules of a bygone age.

The way to release the American economy from dependence upon a continuation of the cold war is to start now the programs of production for peace into which the nation's whole resources can be channeled when peace is achieved.

The same prescription—beginning *now* to produce for the peacetime needs of the world's peoples—provides the only answer to assuring that the American economy will keep pace with Soviet growth.

The American economy is grinding to a halt primarily for two basic reasons: (1) because it has not geared itself to world needs; and (2) because American production has become producer-oriented rather than consumer-oriented.

If the American economy is to remain the bulwark of economic freedom, its emphasis must shift—in private as well as public policy—from profits to people, and not only to those people who happen to be citizens of the United States.

Once the United States deliberately puts itself to work to

satisfy the needs of the world consumer, there will be no danger that American productive capacity will outrun demand. Before this can be done, American business leadership will have to relearn what it once knew and appears to have forgotten: namely, that it is more profitable to make more and better goods for more people at low prices and a small unit margin of profit than to squeeze the maximum profit margin out of each unit sale. The first Henry Ford demonstrated the soundness of this axiom. Pittsburgh and Detroit have reversed the theory of mass production which gave the American economy its greatest impetus. By following a restrictive, producer-oriented policy, American business is pricing both the domestic and the foreign consumer out of the market.

Gearing the American economy to world needs means more than just exporting a surplus of articles made or grown to satisfy the needs or assumed wants of the American people. It means growing foodstuffs specifically needed in food-deficit areas. It means making tools, machinery, and articles of consumption adapted to the requirements of peoples in other lands. It means a public policy of more generous and more understanding aid to world economic development both through the use of public funds and through public incentives to private investment. It means being willing to let other peoples earn dollars by selling their goods in the American market.

None of these requirements will injure the people of the United States. Farmers will be better off growing food to be eaten and fibers to be made into clothing than they are in raising surplus crops to be stored in warehouses, dumped, or destroyed. Factory workers will find new job opportunities far exceeding those lost through foreign competition. The American consumer will enjoy a wider choice of goods at lower prices.

It is true that the shift from economic nationalism to internationalism will require some readjustment. Those industries which cannot live without a high protective tariff may need public assistance in converting to other lines of production in which they can meet foreign competition. Workers temporarily displaced will need unemployment and retraining subsidies. The cost of providing such help will be infinitesimal alongside

73

of the benefits to the consumer, the new job opportunities, and the new fields opened up to business enterprise.

The incentives needed to revitalize the stagnant American economy are basically not new at all. They are the same incentives that originally made America great, before they became stifled within national frontiers which no longer afforded sufficient outlet for humanitarian concern, for the urge to build and create, and for the spirit of adventure. The same energies can be released once more if the American people dedicate a part of their superb productive capacity to satisfying the wants of peoples who not only are not yet surfeited but whose unmet urgent needs create political instability.

To say this is not to advocate political meddling, much less military intervention; in these, the United States has already indulged far too much. Nor is what is here suggested a starry-eyed global share-the-wealth program. What is suggested is neither more nor less than reorienting the American economy toward serving consumers throughout the world. To do so will, to be sure, give purpose and direction to the latent American spirit of humanitarian concern, which is perhaps the best thing that America possesses; but it so happens that what is morally right is also the obvious solution to America's own economic dilemma.

CHAPTER FIVE

Lost Opportunity

At the end of World War II, Germany and Japan, respectively the two great workshops of Europe and Asia, lay prostrate in defeat. Europe, including the Soviet Union, was in a state of physical and moral exhaustion. The British Empire was in the process of disintegration. China was ravaged by war and torn by civil conflict. Hunger stalked the earth, and almost everywhere there was a shortage of every kind of necessity.

Only the United States had, in spite of its great exertions and sacrifices, miraculously emerged from the conflict stronger, more prosperous, and more powerful than ever before. Only the United States was in a position to render substantial aid to relief, reconstruction, and development.

Before the American government became distracted by the postwar political problems to be considered in the next chapter, it rose magnificently to the occasion. The role played by the United States in launching and supporting the United Nations Relief and Reconstruction Administration (UNRRA), the United Nations itself, as well as the World Bank and the International Monetary Fund provides eloquent testimony. The same spirit of responsible helpfulness gave birth later to the Marshall Plan, although by this time (1947) the clouds of the cold war were already gathering.

But when UNRRA was disbanded, when American attention

became focused upon the cold war in Europe, and when the United States became involved in the Chinese civil war, the American government lost sight of what was undoubtedly its greatest postwar opportunity for constructive leadership toward peace. This opportunity lay in Asia, Africa, the Middle East and Latin America, but especially in Asia.

Asian society was in the ferment of a revolutionary change which was soon to spread to other parts of the world.

For centuries past, the conditions of life for that half of the world's population which lived in Asia had been grim and, by Western standards, wholly intolerable. Life expectancy at birth was about thirty years. At least half of an Asian's children normally died before reaching maturity. Most of the Asian people were chained to the land in a never-ending struggle to sustain a bare existence.

Because news had now begun to travel fast into the remotest corners of the earth, the Asian peoples became aware that in other parts of the world men lived an entirely different kind of existence from that to which they had been accustomed. The Asians began to realize that hunger, poverty, disease, and early death were not the immutable fate of man—that elsewhere than in Asia man had been able to emancipate himself from endless toil and grinding poverty.

This newly acquired knowledge gave rise to what has been rightly called the Revolution of Rising Expectations.

For centuries most of Asia had been dominated by white men who came from across the seas to trade, to assert their superior military power, to establish empires, and to quarrel among each other over their special preserves. And then suddenly an Asian nation—Japan—succeeded in driving the Western white man out of Asia.

This event sparked the long-latent Asian Revolution against Colonialism.

When the European white man's power in Asia was broken, the peoples of Asia came to know Japan, their Asian liberator, as a conqueror even more ruthless than their former European overlords. The Chinese, Filipinos, Indonesians, Thais, Malayans, Indochinese, and Burmese, while inclined to be less resentful of an Asian conqueror, discovered nevertheless that being a part of the Nipponese empire was no better and in many ways worse than living under European colonial domination. So that, when the United States—a country which had voluntarily liberated its sole colonial possession in Asia—defeated the Japanese and drove them back to their home islands, the people of Asia were grateful, thinking that now, at last, they would be free.

And this primarily American liberation of Asia from Japanese conquest let loose the Revolution of Asian Nationalism.

If we review United States policy in Asia after World War II, the outstanding fact about it is the failure of the American policy-makers to understand the significance of these three revolutions, which were soon to spread into the Middle East and Africa.

The sad truth is that the United States held the future of most of Asia in its hands and dropped it.

From 1945 to 1955 the United States alone was in a position to render the kind of help that Asia needed. The Soviet Union was as yet in no position to compete. These ten years were almost entirely wasted.

Until 1949 the Truman administration scarcely thought of Asia at all, outside of its special interest in China and Japan. Its major concern was the rehabilitation and defense of a battered and weakened Western Europe.

It was not until 1949 that President Truman inserted a few sentences in his inaugural address announcing "a bold new program of aid to the underdeveloped areas." The President's words echoed around the world and raised high hopes, especially in Asia; but it soon developed that these expectations were doomed to disappointment. The so-called Point Four program turned out to be neither bold nor new. Like the already existing United Nations program, Point Four offered technical advice and assistance, but it provided no financial help to the underdeveloped countries in carrying out whatever technical advice they might accept. It offered what Mr. Truman called "American know-how" without the means of putting it to use. To say this does not minimize the value of technical aid in itself, for such aid alone has in many cases proved helpful. But, on the whole, the spread of technical knowledge without capital assistance served merely to stimulate the Revolution of Rising Expectations without satisfying its demands.

The American Congress did not take kindly to Mr. Truman's modest proposal; for almost a year it wrangled over the pitifully small appropriation requested. Nevertheless, it is quite possible that, had it not been for the outbreak of war in Korea, the launching of the Point Four program might have marked a turning point in United States foreign economic policy. The idea might have been developed into something like a series of Marshall Plans for Asia, Africa, and Latin America. Unhappily, the Korean War created a climate of opinion in which only foreign aid directly related to military strategy received serious consideration. After 1950, by far the largest items in President Truman's foreign aid budgets became those which provided direct and indirect military assistance to the European partners in NATO, to the Republic of Korea, to the exiled Chinese Nationalist regime on Formosa, and to France in Indochina.

When President Eisenhower concluded the Korean armistice, he created the psychological setting in which a new approach to the problems of Asia might have been made. This was the moment when the prestige of the new administration would have permitted it to disengage itself from the internal affairs of China. In the context thus provided, it would have been possible to shift the emphasis from military considerations to constructive economic assistance. Instead, military considerations were given greater emphasis then ever before, and the United States became more deeply committed to the Chinese Nationalists and to a host of new military allies.

For the fiscal year 1954, President Truman had budgeted a total of $7.6 billion for foreign aid. This amount was immediately reduced by President Eisenhower to $5.1 billion and further cut by Congress to $4.5 billion. For 1955, President Eisenhower slashed his request to $3.5 billion, of which Congress granted $2.8 billion. The following year Mr. Eisenhower asked for only $3.2 billion and was granted $2.7 billion. The emphasis in these three Eisenhower budgets remained upon military assistance and so-called defense support, with South Korea, Taiwan, and South Vietnam the chief beneficiaries. Funds for aid to economic development were visible only through a microscope.

By the end of 1955, it became apparent that the Soviet Union was about to launch a major program of economic assistance to the uncommitted countries of Asia. The ten years of American monopoly had ended. The greatest postwar opportunity for American leadership in Asia (and in other parts of the world) had been squandered.

Even then, warnings of Soviet competition and pleas for increased economic aid to the uncommitted and mostly underdeveloped countries failed to move the Eisenhower administration. For the fiscal year ending in June 1957, the President asked for an increase of $2 billion in military aid and defense support, but for only a paltry increase of $200 *million* for economic assistance. The total of American economic aid for the entire world, excluding loans from the Export-Import Bank to finance purchases from the United States, had at this time been reduced to about $300 million per annum.

For the fiscal year ending in June 1958, Congress provided for $130 million in technical assistance and $300 million for a revolving Development Loan Fund, for which the President had asked $750 million. In his 1959 budget, Mr. Eisenhower asked for a total of $3.9 billion, of which more than $3 billion was for military aid and defense support, with $142 million for technical assistance and $625 million for economic development. Congress reduced the latter amount to $400 million and would have cut even deeper had it not been for the crisis in Lebanon and Iraq.

Throughout the postwar period up to the summer of 1958, the American government's annual contribution to the economic development of the underdeveloped countries was less than the amount spent each year by the American people on cosmetics. Future historians—if there are any future historians —may well regard this as the single most important failure of United States postwar policy.

Fortunately there have been marked signs of improvement since the midsummer crisis of 1958. Actually the awakening began somewhat earlier with the appointment of C. Douglas Dillon as Under-Secretary of State for Economic Affairs. In contrast to his ineffective predecessors, Mr. Dillon assumed full responsibility for American foreign economic policy, brought constructive and courageous vision into a field where both had long been lacking, and has been markedly successful in gaining the co-operation of Congress and the Treasury. Nevertheless, it was not until after the Nixon trip to Latin America and the Middle East debacle that Mr. Dillon was able to bring about a partial reversal of American policy with respect to the internationalization of economic aid.

Within a single month—August 1958—President Eisenhower came out in favor of a Middle East Development Authority, an Inter-American Bank, a "soft-loan" subsidiary of the World Bank (the Monroney Plan), and an increase of the lending power of both the World Bank and the International Monetary Fund. The same Congress which had boggled over a niggardly appropriation for the Development Loan Fund had already been quietly persuaded to add $2 billion each to the lending authority of the Export-Import Bank and to the surplus-food-disposal authorization under Public Law 480. These were no mean achievements.

It remained to be seen to what extent this belated reversal of foreign economic policy would be carried into effect and to what extent the new policy could succeed in the context of an as yet unaltered political approach to a world in revolution.

CHAPTER SIX

The Postwar Dilemma of the United States

I

World War II was a coalition war in which, together with their smaller allies, the British, French, Russians, Chinese, and Americans fought, suffered, and contributed to a coalition victory. Therefore, quite naturally, the wartime planning for peace was on a coalition basis; the structure of the United Nations Security Council, the creation of the Council of Foreign Ministers, and the four-power occupation of Germany were all predicated upon the assumption of a coalition-made peace and peace enforcement by a coalition-dominated United Nations.

This proved to be a false assumption. Instead of a world in which power was divided, there came into being for a short time a world in which the United States held what amounted to an effective monopoly of power. In addition to its unique economic position noted in the preceding chapter, the United States found itself in a position of absolute military supremacy not only because of its great army, navy, and air force, but because of its sole possession of the atomic bomb.

Instead of participating in the anticipated coalition-made peace, the United States found itself at loggerheads with the one member of the wartime alliance who still possessed considerable power. At the same time, its other European allies—notably Britain and France—had for the time being become

81

economic wards, while China was rendered impotent by civil conflict.

The first phase of American postwar policy was predicated upon the wartime assumption of a coalition-made peace. This accounts in part at least for the Cairo, Teheran, Yalta, and Potsdam agreements. It also accounts in part for the overhasty demobilization of American military power.

The second phase of American postwar policy consisted of an attempt to adjust to the unexpected split in the coalition and to the equally unexpected paramountcy of American power. This explains the American government's tendency to work single-handed rather than through the United Nations, as for example in China, Japan, Greece, and Turkey. It explains the twists and turns of the Truman Doctrine and the Marshall Plan and, finally, it explains American rearmament.

The policy of military containment was the product of the assumption of American supremacy and the consequent acceptance of global responsibility.

However, by the time this American policy got into full swing, the world had changed once more. Britain and France had regained some measure of economic independence. Russia had made rapid progress in reconstruction and had acquired the secret of the atomic bomb. China had emerged from the civil war with a strong government commanding the greatest military forces in Chinese history. Germany and Japan were beginning to recover from defeat. The United States no longer held a monopoly of power; it now confronted the kind of world it had expected and failed to find in 1945—a world in which power was divided—except that in this second new world, the United States found itself faced by hostile forces of great power, while the friendly forces were relatively weak.

The government of the United States has not yet fully adjusted its foreign policy to the fact that the United States is no longer, as it was for a short moment of history, the paramount power and that, therefore, it can no longer police the world or dictate the conditions of a peaceful settlement.

That, in the opinion of this observer, constitutes one part of the basic dilemma of American diplomacy in the second half of the twentieth century.

The other part of the dilemma is that the government of the United States has not adjusted its policy to the drastic change which has taken place in the nature of physical, economic, and psychological power.

It is now a truism to state that physical force has lost its force as an instrument of national policy, since each side in a world of bipolarized physical power now possesses the means to annihilate the other. It is self-evident that it no longer makes any difference whether one side or the other possesses enough physical force to destroy the other twice over or three times over, so long as the other side is able to retaliate only once with sufficient force.

It is less obvious, but equally true, that economic power has become diluted by the interdependence of the great nation-states; that the United States, for example, is dependent upon other nations for twenty-eight out of thirty-nine industrial minerals essential to national survival. As opposed to the far more self-sufficient Sino-Soviet orbit, the United States must rely for its economic strength upon the co-operation of many other countries, and *this co-operation can be obtained only at a political price*—a price which has gone up steadily as other nations have begun to realize that the United States no longer can spread the umbrella of paramount physical power over them for protection.

These changes in the nature of power mean that an effective American policy must be based more and more upon consent on the part of other nations; that the United States is no longer in a position to demand acquiescence in exchange for protection, but that it must now seek consent through the pursuit of aims which attract the allegiance of other peoples and through a choice of means which command their respect and agreement.

The government of the United States has not yet appreciated either the weakness which accrues from this altered position nor the potential strength vis-à-vis the Sino-Soviet orbit which might accrue from it.

The "weakness" simply stated is that the United States is no longer free to make mistakes, such as those it has committed in the Near and Far East, without losing the adherence of other nations essential to its survival.

The strength of the new position is that the communist dictatorships, because of their self-sufficiency, will be left relatively free to make mistakes such as they have made in Korea and Hungary.

Given an intelligent American policy, based upon a true appraisal of the altered circumstances now prevailing in the world, the net advantage should lie with the United States as against the communist dictatorships. The struggle in which the United States is engaged is, in the last analysis, a struggle for respect in the minds of men—a struggle in which day-to-day world opinion, whether expressed in or outside the United Nations, will play an increasing part. In such a struggle it should be an advantage rather than a disadvantage to be forced by lack of decisive physical power and lack of economic self-sufficiency to take daily account of world opinion.

The great danger to the Western community is that the United States may continue to pursue a policy based upon a no longer existing supremacy of American military and economic power.

II

If one looks back upon American postwar policy, bearing in mind the three basic changes which occurred during this relatively short period, two things seem apparent: *first*, that American policy has consistently lagged behind changing conditions; and, *second*, that American policy has evolved less out of affirmative purpose than out of delayed reaction to unexpected Soviet strength and equally unexpected British weakness.

With the benefit of hindsight, it is easy enough to say that aggressive Soviet expansionism should have been anticipated; that any Russian government, Tsarist or Stalinist, might have been expected to push outward once Germany and Japan, the traditional barriers to Russian expansion into Europe and Asia, had been rendered impotent; and that Stalin would be unlikely to give up the physical control of Eastern Europe acquired in the last stages of the war. At the time, the wartime honeymoon spirit with the Soviet Union understandably beclouded any such realistic anticipation of the future.

Even the shrewdest and most pessimistic observers, however, could scarcely have been expected to foresee that Britain would so soon withdraw from Asia or that Britain's power at home would be so diminished as to make it impossible for her to continue her traditional policy of blocking Russian encroachment southward into the Middle East.

American attention was at first focused upon Stalin's aggressive maneuvers in Eastern Europe and upon the deadlock in Germany resulting from the failure of the four-power occupation of that country. Simultaneously, the United States drifted into an ill-advised entanglement in the Chinese civil war. In both widely separated theaters, the United States developed the determination to stop communism. It was not until March 1947 that the American government became aware of Britain's inability to halt threatened Soviet encroachment in Greece and Turkey. It was at this point that the Truman administration adopted the policy of singlehanded global containment of communism.

Counteraction in Europe was certainly unavoidable. It was also unavoidable that the unique power of the United States be somehow employed in such counteraction. Some observers, the writer among them, felt at the time that United Nations action backed by the United States would have been preferable to unilateral American intervention. Beyond this, however, it did not follow from the need for containment of Soviet expansionism that this should become the sole, overriding aim of American policy or that a policy of containment should take on an ill-conceived and self-defeating form.

The deepening world crisis of 1947 consisted of many elements, most of which had little or nothing to do with the rise of an aggressive Soviet dictatorship nor with an international communist conspiracy, except to some extent in Europe. At this time Stalin had no use for the Chinese communists, contemptuously referring to them as "radishes—red outside but white inside." There was as yet no Sino-Soviet alliance.

Asia was in a state of revolution—against colonialism, against oppression by indigenous ruling cliques, and, above all, against poverty and hunger. Communism was in the process of capturing this revolution in China, not because of Soviet backing but because the West offered no other alternative to the corrupt and inefficient rule of the Kuomintang.

Much the same sort of revolution was latent in Africa and the Middle East.

Europe was drifting toward economic and political chaos—not *because of* the communist conspiracy but ripened nevertheless for communist exploitation by moral and physical exhaustion.

The whole world was in a state of political, military, economic, technological, and psychological change.

In such a world there were bound to be many different sources of danger and many opportunities for constructive action. Yet, when the American policy-makers faced this unfamiliar and rapidly changing world, they saw clearly only one menace to peace and only one threat to American security—namely, the threat of communism. This was clearly stated by President Truman in his message to Congress on March 17, 1948, and repeated at frequent intervals thereafter.

In addition to taking this myopic view of a world in revolution, the Truman administration misread the nature of the one threat to peace which it clearly recognized, believing it to be primarily military rather than political, and directed primarily at Western Europe rather than at Asia and the Middle East. These two assumptions were perhaps natural in view of Stalin's actions in Europe, but they were nevertheless dangerously wrong.

The misreading of the nature and direction of the communist threat led to an excessive preoccupation with Europe—augmented by a justified realization of Europe's urgent need for economic assistance—and to an excessive reliance upon military power. It led, furthermore, to a distortion of American aims and ideals and to a firm disinclination to seek any sort of accommodation with an adversary who was thought to understand no language other than that of military force. Worst of all, this essentially negative, defensive policy left the initiative throughout the postwar period in the hands of the communists.

To round out the legacy of basic misconception inherited and—in spite of campaign oratory—accepted from its predecessor, the Eisenhower administration added two perilously complacent assumptions: (1) that the communist dictatorships would, within the foreseeable future, collapse of their own iniquity and inherent weakness; and (2) that democratic societies would, by their very nature and without any particular effort, always remain far ahead of totalitarian societies in scientific and technological development.

The resulting bipartisan policy has neither contained communism nor brought the world any nearer to peace. The most that can be claimed for it is that it saved Berlin in 1948–49, halted outright military aggression in Korea, and frustrated Soviet designs upon Western Europe. The latter claim rests upon the doubtful assumption that a military attack upon Western Europe was ever contemplated by Soviet leadership.

On the other hand, a futile involvement in the Chinese civil war and global preoccupation with the military means of containment caused neglect of the political aspirations and the economic needs of the emerging peoples. Obsession with armaments and alliances created weakness and dissension in many parts of the so-called free world, rather than unity and strength. It led the United States to arm neighbor against neighbor, in the mistaken belief that it was arming both against a common enemy. It caused the United States, in the name of defending democracy, to ally itself with selfishly oppressive, anti-democratic regimes. All this is, by now, widely recognized.

The tragic irony in the development of American postwar policy was that it rested from the start upon an assumption which the United States itself had invalidated when it opened the door into the atomic age. The first atomic explosion at Alamogordo foreshadowed the end of an era in which military force could serve as an effective instrument of foreign policy. That era came to a definite close in 1949, when the United States lost its atomic monopoly. Yet, throughout the subsequent post-war period, military force has remained the instrument of policy upon which the American government has continued to place its chief reliance.

Having staked its all upon the maintenance of military supremacy, the United States then failed lamentably to accomplish even that objective. Lack of energetic over-all direction by a President supposedly expert in military affairs, inter-service rivalry, false economy, self-defeating secrecy, and, above all, the complacent assumption of Soviet technological inferiority permitted the Russians to overtake the United States in missile development.

Even the dramatic shock of the Soviet sputniks in the autumn of 1957 did not bring about a basic re-examination of American foreign policy. President Eisenhower's January 9, 1958, State of the Union message promised firmer and more vigilant leadership in seeking "safety through strength." It did not foreshadow any reconsideration of the false premises upon which the policy of strength had been developed. Indeed, the President reaffirmed in almost identical words the view which President Truman had expressed ten years earlier.

"The threat to our safety and to the hope of a peaceful world," President Eisenhower said, "is simply stated. It is communist imperialism."

The Chief Executive did at long last recognize that the communist threat was not entirely military, but this verbal modification was accompanied by no new program of action giving greater emphasis to the economic aspects of the cold war. Nor did Mr. Eisenhower convey the slightest hint that he was aware of any revolutionary movements in the world which were neither inspired nor materially influenced by any international communist conspiracy.

Such was the prologue to a year in which the utter bankruptcy of American postwar foreign policy was to be demonstrated by a series of dramatic crises which were to bring the West, if not the entire human race, to the brink of final and complete disaster.

III

It is not intended to repeat or to review here the substance of a long series of newspaper articles, speeches, pamphlets, and books in which this observer has throughout the postwar period expressed his dissent from various aspects of the foreign policy pursued by the Truman and Eisenhower administrations. Nor would any useful purpose be served by recalling the alternative policies from time to time proposed with respect to most of the areas in which the crises of 1958 brought matters to a head. This chapter is concerned not with what might have been done in the past but with that which might still be done now and in the future.

Prior to the French-Algerian, Middle Eastern, and Far Eastern crises of 1958, it was possible for a critic of Western policy to suggest clearly defined alternative courses of action. Since then it has become very much more difficult to visualize the future; but, in spite of the uncertainties created by recent developments, it remains more than ever necessary to attempt, where at all possible, to see how the past shortcomings of Western policy might be corrected.

Irrespective of the extent to which the reader may agree or disagree with what has been said about Western policy up to this point, the fact is that the West now faces a radically changed situation. Whether past policy has been wise or ill conceived, ably or badly executed, most of it is now irrelevant.

The central elements in the new and unfamiliar world of the second postwar decade, which has been emerging far more rapidly than anyone expected, are:

1. The rise of China as a third super-power.
2. The rise of nationalism, in both the old-established and the newly independent nations.
3. The rise of neutralism.
4. The growing tendency of the newly independent peoples to fall into various patterns of authoritarianism, not by any means necessarily of the communist variety.

To be sure, the cold war continues, having become something of an economic necessity for the West and a political necessity for the communist dictatorships. Washington and Moscow continue their debates, their maneuvers and countermaneuvers, and their insane armaments race, keeping all of the world's peoples face to face with the threat of annihilation. China is becoming an ever more dangerous third element in this explosive situation. But in spite of all this—and perhaps to a great extent because of it—the world's peoples are more and more turning their backs upon the three great protagonists. Washington, Moscow, and Peking are becoming increasingly isolated in a psychotic atmosphere of their own making.

The center of the stage is now held by new forces.

Ten years ago it was the generally accepted doctrine that only the United States could save the "free world" from communism. Until the final rout of the Nationalist armies and the flight of Chiang Kai-shek to Taiwan, there was little non-communist criticism of American intervention in the Chinese civil conflict. Europe was preoccupied with its own affairs and in dire need of assistance in recovering from the ravages of war and in staving off economic and political chaos.

Wherever there was trouble—and there was trouble almost everywhere throughout the non-communist world—American intervention was not only gladly accepted but eagerly sought. Peoples emerging or seeking to emerge into national independence looked to the United States for assistance in liberating themselves and in developing their national economies. American intervention on a global basis was held to be more than altruism; it was regarded as enlightened self-interest not only by the beneficiaries and would-be beneficiaries but in the United States itself. It seemed logical to think of a "free-world" coalition led by the United States and equally logical for the United States to think that its own frontiers extended as far as the boundary between the communist orbit and the "free world."

All that has changed.

Western Europe has regained its economic health and, with it, a measure of political independence. It no longer greatly fears a Soviet attack across the Elbe and the Rhine. Almost every

European nation has its own preoccupations which override its interest in the NATO alliance: France in North Africa; Britain in Aden and the Persian Gulf; Britain, Greece, and Turkey in Cyprus; and Germany in its own reunification.

The emerging peoples of Asia and the Middle East have learned that the American help they had hoped for was to be obtained only—or almost only—for the purposes of rearmament and at the price of becoming the military allies of the United States in a coalition which seemed to them more likely to provoke war than to prevent it. Worse yet, they have gained the impression that the United States opposes the revolutionary changes to which they are committed; that, in the American concept of the "free world," only one freedom—freedom from communism—seems greatly to matter.

The forces which today rule the "free world" are the centrifugal forces of old and new nationalism, rather than the centripetal forces of internationalism based upon common fear or common purpose.

In these circumstances, American intervention is no longer welcome, unless its purpose coincides with indigenous nationalistic aims and aspirations. France has wanted no American intervention in North Africa, unless it were to support "Algérie Française"; the Algerians have wanted no American intervention, unless it were to back their demand for independence. Britain wants no American meddling in the Persian Gulf area, unless it supports her interests; and the Arabs want the United States to keep out of the Middle East, unless Washington will align itself with Arab nationalism at the expense of Britain and Israel.

Granted that nationalism is anachronistic in an age when reason and increasing economic interdependence demand that the world unite in common interest, the facts of rampant nationalism are inescapable. The driving forces behind nationalism are the quest for recognized independence and equality and the determination to achieve social and economic betterment.

This may not be the world we would like to see developing, but it is the world that exists for the time being.

Intervention, whether by the U.S. or the U.S.S.R., is now suspect. Anti-communism is no longer an overriding interest anywhere, except in Taipei, Seoul, Madrid, and Washington.

In this new and unfamiliar world, American intervention makes sense, if at all, only when clearly understood vital interests of the United States are at stake and when these interests coincide with the aspirations of the people—not necessarily the government—native to the area concerned. This means that the United States should, in its own interest, desist from global meddling, cut down its far-flung commitments, and re-examine carefully what its own vital interests actually are.

To say this is not to advocate an isolationist policy. Nor is it to renounce humanitarian interest in the welfare of other peoples or to give up resistance to communist aggression. What is called for is not a retreat into "Fortress America" but a reappraisal of existing alliances and commitments. Such a reappraisal would probably result in a reduced emphasis upon Europe and an increased emphasis—though not in terms of military alliances—upon Asia, Africa, and Latin America. It would result in the realization that European interests are perhaps inevitably involved in the maintenance or attempted restoration of the traditional *status quo,* whereas American interests actually lie in the direction of guiding change into constructive channels.

Again, this does not mean abandoning NATO or ceasing to maintain an interest in the reunification of Germany or in the eventual liberation of the East European satellites. It does mean recognizing that these aims are no longer separable from an over-all relaxation of tensions through political settlements and from bringing the arms race to a halt. It means recognizing that NATO is in one sense an encumbrance when it comes to give-and-take negotiation with Moscow, because the interests of all the European partners are not identical and often conflict with the interests of the United States.

A second conclusion derives from the observation that all the conflicting nationalisms in the new and unfamiliar world increasingly have one thing in common; namely, fear of nuclear war between the United States and Russia. This fear creates increasing resentment against both of the super-powers, an attitude of "a plague on both your houses"—in other words, neutralism.

Nor is it only the fear of war and resentment against those who might provoke it that creates neutralism. Belonging to a military alliance is seen, especially by many of the newly independent nations, as an infringement of national sovereignty. People tend to resent the possibility of being forced into action, particularly military action, by the decision of another country. This is true even in the United States.

Neutralism is by no means confined to those countries—such as India, Yugoslavia, and the United Arab Republic—whose governments openly avow a policy of non-alignment. Neutralism is a rapidly growing sentiment within many of the countries whose governments have entered into one or more of the many military alliances sponsored by the United States, as witness the popular uprising against the pro-Western government of Iraq.

Moreover, there is a strong element of neutralism in countries whose governments firmly adhere to the anti-communist alliance, as for example in the British Labour Party, in the West German Social Democratic opposition, and in various segments of French public opinion. One might even say that the apparent apathy of many Americans toward questions of foreign policy is due to something very like neutralism. This sentiment does not imply impartiality as between communism and anti-communism; it expresses disillusioned disinterest in what appears to be a dangerous and apparently sterile power struggle.

In the new world of the latter half of the twentieth century, the United States and the other Western governments will have to take a new look at both nationalism and neutralism. They will have to lay aside their preconceptions, seek to understand these two powerful forces, and find a way of coming to terms with them.

A corollary conclusion, almost too obvious to mention, is that neither nationalist revolution nor neutralist sentiment can be stemmed by military force. John L. Lewis once remarked, when a strike of his coal miners was threatened by the use of troops: "They'll find out that they can't mine coal with bayonets"—a truth which the French had discovered during their occupation of the German Ruhr after World War I. The Western powers will have to learn that they cannot make foreign policy with bayonets either—nor, for that matter, with nuclear bombs.

In dealing with nationalism and neutralism in the non-communist world, the Russians enjoy the advantage that they gain ground by doing little or nothing, whereas, by doing nothing, the Western powers steadily lose ground. The Marxist-Leninist doctrine teaches that nationalist revolution is a first step toward communism. The more such revolutions disrupt the non-communist world, the better the Russians like it. Hence, it has been a simple matter for the Kremlin to encourage nationalism, to appear as the friend of the emerging peoples, and —for the time being—to respect their neutralism.

The Russians enjoy this advantage only because the West has adopted the Marxist-Leninist theory that nationalism is a first step toward communism and therefore a force inherently hostile to Western interests. Actually, this is true only if the West foolishly considers its interests to lie in the maintenance of the *status quo*. Nationalism need not by any means necessarily lead to communism, unless it is driven into the arms of communism by such shortsighted Western policies as those of the French in Indochina.

Furthermore, the Soviet attitude is reversed when it comes to nationalism and neutralism within the communist orbit, as witness Tito, Gomulka, and Imre Nagy. In the face of Soviet repression of nationalism and neutralism within the Sino-Soviet empire, the myth of Soviet friendship for the emerging peoples of the non-communist world is sustained only by the foolishness of the West in fighting history instead of getting into step with it.

Another aspect of the same question concerns the dogmatic attitude of the West, and especially of the United States, toward "democracy" and "capitalism." If the West, and particularly the United States, would try to understand history instead of fighting it, it would be recognized that the emerging peoples can work toward political and economic freedom only through a period of strong centralization of political authority and economic control. This has been the history to date of the

Turkish and Mexican revolutions. It might well have been the history of the Sun Yat-sen revolution had the Kuomintang not become infected with corruption.

There is at the very least a potential difference between an authoritarian dictatorship which emerges as the first step out of feudalism and an authoritarian rule which results from the overthrow or decay of a democracy. An Atatürk, a Nasser, and even a Tito may conceivably, by accident or design, prepare the ground for democracy; in the long run, a dictatorship which sets out to raise the level of a backward people almost inevitably tends to mellow. This is not true of a regressive dictatorship such as that of Franco in Spain or of Trujillo in the Dominican Republic. The distinction is often lost upon an American leadership which desires to help a world-wide evolution toward democracy but which is actually more concerned with the maintenance of things as they are.

Under the influence of the United States, the West is being defeated by its own fears. It is being defeated not in the arsenals and science laboratories of the Soviet Union but in the minds and hearts of the world's peoples. It is being defeated not by the strength and skill of its communist adversaries but by its own failure to understand history, by its lack of empathy and imagination, by its callous indifference to humanity, and by its fear-inspired clinging to the *status quo* in a period of rapid and ineluctable change.

IV

What, then, can be done?

In this observer's opinion, two basic conditions must be recognized and two major efforts must be launched simultaneously:

1. It must be recognized that the arms race is suicidal madness, irrespective of whether the United States is ahead or behind in this senseless competition; and that the number-one task is not how to win the arms race but how to end it.

2. The United States and its allies have, so far, clung to the notion that the communist dictatorships could be forced,

95

bluffed, or frightened into making one-sided concessions or withdrawals, refusing to admit the proven bankruptcy of their policy of declining to negotiate except from "a position of strength." It must now be recognized that the sole alternative to suicidal conflict—or to the indefinite protraction of a condition in which such a conflict may at any moment be precipitated— is give-and-take negotiation of outstanding disputes on the basis of mutually recognized parity (or stalemate) of power.

No one has stated the need for such negotiation more eloquently than Canada's former Foreign Minister, Lester B. Pearson, in a speech delivered in New York on January 11, 1958. After pointing to the frozen rigidity of both American and Soviet diplomacy, Mr. Pearson said:

> It is essential that we avoid this kind of dangerous stalemate in international policy . . .
>
> What is needed is a new and vigorous determination to use every technique of discussion and negotiation that may be available; or, more important, that can be made available for the solution of the tangled, frightening problems that divide today, in fear and hostility, the two power-blocs and thereby endanger peace. We must keep on trying to solve problems one by one, stage by stage, if not on the basis of confidence and co-operation, at least on one of mutual toleration and self-interest.
>
> What I plead for is no spectacular meeting of a Big Two or a Big Three or a Big Four at the summit, where the footing is precarious and the winds blow hard, but for frank, serious and complete exchange of views—especially between Moscow and Washington—through diplomatic and political channels . . .
>
> A diplomatic approach of this kind involves, I know, baffling complexities, difficulties and even risks. Nevertheless, the greater these are, the stronger should be the resolve and the effort by both sides in direct discussions to identify and expose them as the first step in their possible removal . . .
>
> The time has come for us to make a move, not only from

strength but from wisdom and from confidence in ourselves; to concentrate on the possibilities of agreement,
rather than on the disagreements and failures, the evils and
and wrongs of the past.

It would be folly to expect quick, easy or total solutions.
It would be folly also to expect hostility and fears suddenly
to vanish. But it is equal or even greater folly to do nothing;
to sit back, answer missile with missile, insult with insult
and ban with ban.

That would be the complete bankruptcy of policy and
diplomacy, and it would not make for peace . . .

If the truth of Mr. Pearson's remarks is recognized by the
American government—as it certainly should be after the disastrous experiences of 1958—it will become apparent that the
field for give-and-take negotiation falls into two broad areas:
(1) the shaping of a stepwise procedure toward halting the
arms race and eventually bringing about full, universal disarmament; and (2) the relaxation of existing tensions through
political settlements of the major outstanding disputes.

In the writer's opinion, these two aims are interdependent and
require simultaneous, parallel efforts.

CHAPTER SEVEN

Disarmament

The so-called disarmament talks, desultorily carried on to date, have been unrealistic in a number of respects:

1. They have been conducted in a political vacuum—that is to say, without a simultaneous sincere effort to settle the political differences which originally provoked the arms race and which continue to sustain it.

2. They have been conducted without the participation of China—in fact, as if the strongest military power in Asia did not exist, and as if universal national disarmament could be achieved without the slightest consultation with a government which rules one quarter of the world's population.

3. The proposals put forward have been advanced as "first steps" toward disarmament without any attempt to answer the question: "First steps toward what?" There has been no definition of the goal toward which these "first steps" were to lead, nor any plan for a stepwise procedure toward its realization.

4. The negotiations carried on to date have actually not been about disarmament but about a limitation and control of armaments, aimed more at limiting war than at abolishing it altogether. The underlying assumption has been that, while neither side could trust the other to carry out disarmament without "foolproof" inspection and enforcement, it might be possible to keep any future wars within the limits of previously

made agreements. This, in the writer's opinion, is an assumption worthy of Lewis Carroll.

5. The truth of the matter is that neither the United States nor the Soviet Union has been seriously seeking to abolish war. Each side has sought to improve its own position in the event of war by seeking to impose such limitations as would work in its favor. Soviet leadership, knowing that it possesses preponderance in trained manpower and conventional armaments, has sought to obtain a ban on nuclear weapons. The United States and its allies, having "conventionalized" nuclear weapons in order to offset the Soviet advantage without making the costly and painful effort of raising huge armies, have endeavored to insure themselves against surprise nuclear attack without abolishing their own nuclear armaments. Hence the Soviet leadership has in effect been talking about nuclear disarmament without more than a minimum of inspection, while the Western powers have been talking about inspection without more than a minimum of disarmament.

6. Neither side has as yet been prepared to renounce force as the ultimate method of settling disputes. Each wants to retain "deterrent power" of one sort or another.

On the other hand, there are certain elements of reality underlying the sporadic negotiations which have been carried on:

1. Both sides are afraid of and anxious to avoid a major conflict, knowing that in such a conflict the victor will probably be indistinguishable from the vanquished.

2. Both sides are aware of the growing danger that a nuclear war may be triggered by accident.

3. Both sides are staggering under the ever-growing burden of the arms race and anxious to reduce its costs.

4. Each side fears that a point may be reached at which the other may prefer to run even the risks of a nuclear holocaust rather than endure the intolerable burdens and tensions of a continued arms race.

5. Both sides are increasingly aware of the pressure of world opinion—including opinion in their own countries—demanding an end to the arms race and to the threat of extinction.

99

If the human race is to survive, there is no alternative to the ultimate establishment of peace through world law. The writer has long believed that war can and must eventually be abolished altogether through total, universal disarmament, enforced by a reorganized United Nations authorized and empowered by all the world's peoples to compel the peaceable settlement of disputes among the nation-states.

The world's greatest present need is for the education of peoples and governments both as to the urgent necessity for the abolition of war through disarmament and as to its practical feasibility. A major contribution in this direction has been made by the eminent lawyer, Grenville Clark, in association with Professor Louis B. Sohn of Harvard University, in putting forward for discussion a concrete plan for so amending the United Nations Charter as to make the world organization capable of enforcing universal national disarmament.[1] Charles S. Rhyne, president of the American Bar Association, has further emphasized the need for creating adequate machinery for the worldwide peaceable adjudication of international disputes, recommending that the little-used International Court of Justice be immediately integrated with the United Nations and augmented by a system of regional circuit courts.[2]

While it is imperative that the education of world opinion proceed with maximum speed, the fact remains that at present neither the United States nor the Soviet Union is prepared to accept the full implication of universal, enforced disarmament. Neither is as yet ready to recognize the primacy of the United Nations.

The United States has treated the United Nations with cavalier arrogance, attempting to substitute itself for the world organization as a self-appointed, global guardian. Secretary Dulles has never believed in a strong United Nations, conceiving of the world organization as "a town meeting of the world," and placing his reliance for the preservation of peace not upon the United Nations but upon regional military alli-

[1]Clark and Sohn, *World Peace through World Law*, Harvard, 1958.

[2]Rhyne, *Address to the American Bar Association*, August 25, 1958.

ances. We have his own word for it that it was he who labored long and hard at Dumbarton Oaks and San Francisco to bring Article 51 into the Charter. The Dulles concept of a toothless United Nations, as opposed to President Roosevelt's concept of a Charter "with teeth in it," did not derive from Soviet abuse of the veto in the Security Council; it was inherent in Mr. Dulles's attitude long before the United Nations came into being. During his incumbency as Secretary of State, the only times Mr. Dulles has been willing to appeal to the United Nations have been when he literally did not know what else to do, on occasions such as the Soviet intervention in Hungary or the two Middle East crises, largely produced by his own blundering diplomacy. In fairness one must add that neither President Truman nor Mr. Acheson, his last Secretary of State, had any great respect for the United Nations, as witness their predilection for unilateral action.

As for the Soviet Union, the Kremlin has defied the United Nations, obstructed its working, flouted the obligations embodied in its Charter, and used the world organization merely as a sounding board for its propaganda. However, without excusing any part of Soviet behavior, it is only fair to remember that throughout most of the postwar period Russia has faced a hostile majority in the United Nations, whereas the United States has, until recently, been able to count upon a friendly majority.

Other nations too—notably Britain, France, and India—have refused to let the United Nations deal with matters which they have considered their private concern but which have clearly affected many other nations and constituted a threat to world peace. Cyprus, Kashmir, and Algeria are examples. Furthermore, Britain, France, and Israel violated their Charter obligations when they invaded Egypt in 1956.

Since the necessary Charter revision would undoubtedly involve a modification of the present form of representation—under which each nation, no matter what its size or importance, has one vote—it is unlikely that in the existing state of world affairs a two-thirds majority could be mustered for Charter amendment. The smaller nations would, at present, see in such a change a diminution of their power and a threat to their independence.

All these various national attitudes must change before there can be any realistic hope of universal disarmament. The simple fact is that the world is in a perilous period of transition from a system of fully sovereign nation-states to a system of supranational world organization.

This transition cannot be fully accomplished until the majority of the world's peoples and governments agree that there must be supranational machinery to guarantee that inevitable social and political change shall be accomplished peaceably under law. Disarmament assumes either that there will be no change—which is absurd—or that change can be brought about without violence. The greatest obstacle standing in the way of the second assumption is that the communists expect inevitable change to create a communist world, while the Western nations think they can live only in a world which will eventually become one great, open society. Stated in other terms, communist dictatorship is aggressively allied to the change which it wants and considers inevitable, while the West tends to equate the rule of law with the maintenance of the *status quo*—or, at the very least, with resistance to change in the direction of communism.

In the meantime there has been developing, even under the present Charter provisions, something that in many ways resembles a rudimentary world government or, perhaps more accurately stated, a rudimentary world democracy.

Power in the United Nations has gradually shifted away from both the United States and the Soviet Union and toward the uncommitted nations. The "Uniting for Peace Resolution," sponsored by the United States during the Korean War, transferred a considerable measure of power from the Security Council to the General Assembly, thus substantially diluting the Soviet Union's ability to obstruct action. On the other hand, the admission of a score of new members has changed the complexion of the Assembly, so that the United States can no longer count upon an automatic majority and finds itself compelled to bargain for support among friendly nations, neutral nations, and nations whose friendship it would like to acquire. Thus something like a two-thirds-majority rule is beginning to take shape in the world organization. The difficulty is that, while United Nations action is increasingly representative of the will of the majority of member-states, this majority is not representative of the world's peoples and cannot become so as long as the rule of "one nation, one vote" remains in effect. Nevertheless, what has been happening almost imperceptibly is that at every important turn of events the big powers have found it necessary to shape their conduct in such a way as to gain the support of the smaller nations.

In which direction this interesting development will lead—whether toward or away from a truly representative world government—it is impossible to predict. Whatever the future political developments, one thing is certain: the economic pressures toward world unification are going to increase.

Coming back to the more specific question of disarmament, there is considerable disagreement as to whether or not any substantial progress in that direction must wait upon the settlement of major disputes and upon a major change in national attitudes. Many competent observers hold the view that it is idle to discuss disarmament until the underlying causes of the arms race have been eliminated. Philip Noel Baker, the veteran British internationalist, has made a persuasive case for the belief that disarmament itself would relieve most of the political tensions which now keep the world in turmoil.[3]

The writer does not view the matter as an either-or question, believing that some change of attitude and some relaxation of tension are preconditions for disarmament, and that disarmament itself, when achieved, will prove to be the greatest single solvent of fear and hostility. Hence simultaneous efforts in both directions will tend to complement and reinforce each other.

The writer has further contended that negotiated disengagement will provide a practical approach to disarmament; that

[3]Philip Noel Baker, *The Arms Race*, Stephens (London), 1958.

neutralizing the major potential areas of conflict will not only relax tensions but create testing grounds for United Nations inspection and enforcement; and that disengagement—if accomplished in time—will prevent the nuclear armament of countries, such as the two German states, which would lie within the neutralized zones.

The banning of nuclear test explosions—in any case a moral imperative—would further restrict the spread throughout the world of nuclear weapons. An agreement among the nuclear powers to embargo nuclear weapons as well as all materials and information pertinent to their manufacture would reinforce a ban on test explosions.

These are practical steps which could have been taken and might still be taken now, and which would result both in a relaxation of tensions and in progress toward halting the arms race.

Unhappily, the situation rapidly deteriorated during 1958. The prospects for disengagement were dimmed at least temporarily by the Western debacle in the Middle East and by the renewed conflict in the Far East over the Chinese offshore islands. The slow but steady progress toward an agreement to ban nuclear test explosions received a setback through General de Gaulle's insistence that France must become a nuclear power. The revelation of the extent to which negligence, incompetence, false economy and complacency had permitted the United States to fall behind in missile development and in air defense opened up the prospect of a period of years, beginning in 1960, during which the Soviet Union might quite likely enjoy a steadily increasing superiority in nuclear striking power.

Optimistically, one could assume that Soviet leadership would exploit such a period of nuclear ascendancy by its own version of "brinkmanship" rather than by an attempt to destroy the retaliatory power of the United States in a sudden attack. (Even this prospect of nibbling tactics backed by what President Eisenhower called "ballistic blackmail" is grim enough.) However, once China becomes a nuclear power, it can by no means be taken for granted that the Mao regime will be similarly restrained. Nor can it be taken for granted that, if the United

States should regain parity with the Soviet Union, a new disparity will not be created by Chinese entry into the nuclear weapons race.

In any event, it seems reasonably certain that the whole strategy of nuclear war will change when manned bombers and liquid-fueled rockets launched from highly vulnerable fixed bases are supplanted by solid-fueled missiles whose launching sites will presumably be mobile, difficult to detect, and more or less invulnerable. Whether disarmament enforced by foolproof inspection will then still be possible seems open to doubt.

The terrible danger facing the world as this book goes to press is that during the relatively short time when enforced disarmament may still be technically possible, neither side will seriously try to achieve it—that Soviet leadership will seek to exploit and maintain its advantage, while Western leadership will put off negotiation until something like nuclear parity has been restored. Here lies the clearly marked road to disaster. . . .

If there remains any capacity for rational thought in Moscow, Peking and the Western capitals, surely it should be apparent that the time has come to halt this madness—at least to the extent of banning further test explosions and preventing the wider distribution of nuclear weapons. Only thus can a breathing space be gained in which to negotiate the political settlements which are a precondition to universal disarmament under world law.

In the last analysis, the question of nuclear warfare has become a moral problem for the individual, rather than merely a problem for governments, and particularly for those individuals who live in a free, democratic society. It has become a problem which cannot be delegated and which each individual must ultimately face.

CHAPTER EIGHT

The 1958 Crises and the Prospects for Disengagement

I

The term "disengagement" came into prominence in 1957 chiefly through the public discussion between former Secretary of State Acheson and his former chief planner, George F. Kennan. Unfortunately this debate served more to generate heat than to shed light.

Mr. Kennan's advocacy of disengagement in Europe through the neutralization of Germany and a mutual withdrawal of Western and Soviet troops was not only somewhat imprecise but also weakened by that part of the context of his Reith Lectures which seemed to suggest a policy of indifference and aloofness with regard to the uncommitted nations of Asia, Africa, and the Middle East. Coming from the author of the policy of containment, the Reith Lectures nevertheless created something of a sensation, especially as their scholarly serenity presented a welcome relief from the prevailing type of discussion.

Regrettably, Mr. Acheson chose to answer his former associate in rather harsh polemical terms, picking upon certain obvious minor flaws in Mr. Kennan's presentation and putting forward a militant defense of the European policy which he himself had initiated, which Mr. Dulles had adopted, and which had obviously run into a dead-end street.

Where Mr. Kennan's case suffered from the lack of bringing an interesting philosophy down to a specific proposal, Mr. Acheson's rebuttal displayed little more than his well-known debating skill without offering anything new with respect to a situation which clearly required rethinking.

Actually there was nothing new in Mr. Kennan's proposal in so far as it concerned disengagement in Europe. The idea of neutralizing Germany and gradually creating a militarily neutralized belt in Central Europe has been discussed here and abroad for the past ten years.[1] In fact, one of Mr. Acheson's curious arguments against his former associate was that he had had an opportunity to present his views within the department years ago and that they had been rejected. (As if this proved either that Mr. Kennan had been wrong then or that he could not possibly be right years later.)

Because of the confusion which has arisen over the whole question of disengagement, it may be useful to define at least what this writer has had in mind in urging that the United States pursue a policy of disengagement not only in Europe but wherever there is a dangerous confrontation of hostile forces.

To pursue a policy of disengagement means to explore every possibility of converting areas of potential conflict into neutralized zones, preferably placed wherever possible under United Nations supervision. Such supervision would not imply guardianship. It would imply nothing more than the function of seeing to it that whatever agreements may be reached in the various areas are carried out.

There are two kinds of areas of potential conflict between the Western powers and the Sino-Soviet dictatorships:

(a) An area where the opposing forces each have hold of a part of what used to be one country and are tugging, like two dogs at a bone, each trying to pull the whole away from the other. Germany, Korea, and Vietnam are examples.

[1]See the author's *Germany—Bridge or Battleground,* Harcourt Brace, 1947; *Last Call for Common Sense,* Harcourt Brace, 1949; *Germany—Key to Peace,* Harvard University Press, 1953.

(b) An area in which one side holds a position of dominance challenged by the other and objected to by the people of the area itself. The outstanding examples are the Soviet position in Eastern Europe and the Western position—or what now remains of it—in the Arab Middle East.

With respect to the first category, the writer has long maintained that these unhappily partitioned countries can be reunited and eliminated as bones of contention only through a mutual withdrawal of the contending outsiders and a mutual agreement on their part to respect the reunited countries' military neutralization and political independence. This involves the voluntary acceptance of such a status by the countries concerned. Austria provides an example of this sort of settlement.

Germany is the key to the reunification of Europe through a policy of disengagement. The neutralization of Germany, involving the retirement of foreign forces from German soil, would, however, entail far-reaching consequences in Poland, Czechoslovakia, Hungary, and possibly Rumania. It is probable that the Soviet Union would accept these consequences if the United States and Britain would agree to withdraw their troops from the European Continent altogether. The Russians have, in fact, several times proposed just this, agreeing that, in such an event, they would withdraw their own forces behind the Soviet frontier.[2] In the existing circumstances, the Western powers could not, however, be expected to agree to an Anglo-American withdrawal across the Channel. They could, at most, take a first tentative step in that direction by agreeing to withdraw from Germany—perhaps only as far as the west bank of the Rhine—in exchange for a Soviet withdrawal from East Germany.

Recognizing that the only practicable first step toward disengagement in Central Europe would involve a dis-proportionately large Soviet sacrifice, the writer suggested that disengagement in Europe be combined with simultaneous disengagement

[2]See the Soviet Note of November 17, 1956, in the *New York Times*, November 18, 1956.

in the Middle East, where the Western powers had more to give up than the Soviet Union.[3]

This proposal was based upon the conviction that both the Soviet position in Eastern Europe and the Western position in the Middle East were ultimately untenable, because both were imposed upon the native populations against their own aims and aspirations. Thus it seemed logical and perhaps practical to envisage an arrangement under which each side would, without loss of face, be able to retreat from an ultimately untenable position—the disproportionately large Soviet withdrawal in Europe being balanced against a Western retreat from an area where the West still had a number of military and other assets, whereas the Soviet Union had only a recently acquired political bridgehead.

The events of the summer of 1958 have, for the time being, destroyed the possibility of such a solution. Prior to their occurrence, it might have been possible for the West to obtain disengagement in Europe by trading off the ill-conceived Baghdad Pact in exchange for a mutual hands-off agreement under which both sides would refrain from interference in the internal affairs of the Middle Eastern states and agree not to ship arms into the area. (Turkey could have been excluded from such an agreement because of its membership in NATO.) Both sides might have agreed to co-operate in trying to establish peace between the Arab states and Israel and to work together in aiding the economic development of the entire area.

The Polish and Hungarian revolts in the autumn of 1956 created the opportunity for putting forward such a proposal, but, while the Western powers failed to take advantage of the Soviet difficulties in Eastern Europe, the Soviet government lost no time in taking advantage of Western troubles in the Middle East. In its note of February 11, 1957,[4] the Kremlin seized the initiative in making a proposal for disengagement in the Middle East, including an arms embargo, non-interference

[3]This was the main theme of the author's *Agenda for Action—Toward Peace through Disengagement,* Monde Publishers, 1957.

[4]See *New York Times* of February 12, 1957.

in the internal affairs of the Arab states, co-operation in economic development, and withdrawal of military bases and forces.

The trouble with this proposal was that, not being linked to a Soviet withdrawal in Eastern Europe, it was obviously a one-sided affair. Nevertheless, it opened the door to negotiation.

Instead of accepting the Soviet proposals in principle, provided that they be combined with a first step toward disengagement in Germany, Washington brushed off the overture as "insincere propaganda designed merely to make trouble for the Eisenhower Doctrine." Thus another opportunity was lost. The United States and Great Britain still persisted in the notion that the Soviet Union could be treated as an outsider with no legitimate interests in the Middle East, and that further Soviet intrusion could be prevented by making military allies out of a few feudal regimes already clearly foredoomed to be engulfed by the rising tide of revolution.

II

The revolt against the pro-Western governments of Iraq, Lebanon, and Jordan in July 1958 destroyed the Anglo-American illusion. Forced on the defensive, the Western powers were now compelled to do precisely what the Russians had wanted them to do a year earlier; namely, to retreat from the Middle East without obtaining a Soviet retreat from Eastern Europe.

On July 16, 1958, two days after the American marines landed in Lebanon, a speech was made on the floor of the Senate to which the administration might well have given heed. Senator J. W. Fulbright of Arkansas took this occasion to discuss what seemed to him the underlying causes of the failure of American policy not only in the Middle East but elsewhere.

Mr. Fulbright noted, in the first place, that the United States appeared to lack any "long-range policy to serve as a guide to day-to-day decisions." Specifically, as to the Middle East, he said that the American government had "never made the fundamental policy decisions as to whether Arab nationalism—epitomized in Nasser—was a force with which we should try to work or a force which we should oppose. As a consequence," the Senator said, "our day-to-day actions have vacillated between tempting Arab nationalism with offers of assistance . . . and taunting it with refusals to sell wheat or to continue CARE programs and other petty annoyances."

Secondly, the Senator observed that in the Middle East, as elsewhere, the United States had "relied on military pacts and doctrines without relation to the question whether the dangers involved were of a military nature, or whether their solution was possible by military means." He suggested that "the pat military answers" of the Baghdad Pact and the Eisenhower Doctrine actually "obscured the basic problems and postponed their solution . . . Reliance upon military means," Mr. Fulbright said, had "caused us to lose touch with the ordinary people." This did not apply only to the Middle East. "In few of the newly independent countries," Mr. Fulbright said, "have we an understanding of the motivations of the common man." In the Middle East, "the United States has dealt with princes, potentates, big businessmen and the entrenched, frequently corrupt representatives of the past."

Finally, the Arkansan remarked that the United States appeared to recognize "only one brand of revolution—that which is directed by communism . . . There is a question," he said, "whether we have not become so obsessed with our fear of communism that we are unable to appraise the motivation of such violent revolutions as are occurring in the Middle East."

Being a loyal Democrat, Mr. Fulbright did not say that the basic defects of United States postwar policy which he now recognized had been inherent in President Truman's policies long before the Eisenhower administration had taken office. Yet it was extremely important to realize that such had been the case; for, to blame this policy solely upon a Republican administration was likely to prejudice the unbiased evaluation to which the Senator's penetrating criticism was entitled.

Unfortunately there were no indications whatever that either President Eisenhower or his Secretary of State recognized the truth of Senator Fulbright's observations.

The following passage is quoted from Mr. Arthur Krock's column in the *New York Times* of July 18, 1958:

> In the meeting of Congressional leaders with the President [on Monday, July 14, the day before the marines landed] the Senator [Fulbright] asked some questions which projected his thought that obsession with international communism may blind our authorities to other sources of revolution. But in reply the President and Secretary Dulles were positive that the violence in Lebanon and Iraq was inspired and supplied by a Nasser-Soviet combination of mutual interest.

Now the revolts in Lebanon, Jordan, and Iraq were unquestionably influenced by the example set by Gamal Abdel Nasser. They were, no doubt, openly encouraged by propaganda from Cairo and Moscow. There was undoubtedly some infiltration into Lebanon by Syrian bands and some supply of small arms from Syria to the Lebanese rebels.

But when the President and Mr. Dulles made the statement reported by Mr. Krock, they were well aware that the United Nations observers had reported that outside influence was *not* playing a major part in the rebellion against the Chamoun government. Until they were caught by surprise, on July 14, by the sudden and successful revolution in Iraq, the President and Mr. Dulles had, in fact, welcomed the United Nations report as a valid reason for *not* sending troops to Lebanon. It was the sudden overthrow of the pro-Western Iraqi government—not the state of affairs in Lebanon—which caused the emergency meeting with the congressional leaders and the decision, apparently not disclosed at the meeting, to undertake military intervention. At the time there was not a shred of evidence that the revolt in Iraq had been "inspired and supplied" either by Cairo or Moscow. In fact, there was no information whatever, except that which came from the Baghdad radio.

Subsequently it was learned that the coup in Iraq had been brought off by a small clique of army officers, much as General Naguib and Colonel Nasser had managed to overthrow King

Farouk in Egypt in 1952. The Egyptian example may well have "inspired" this action, but the important fact was that the coup had the instant and almost unanimous support of the Iraqi population. The army officers had obviously merely triggered a latent revolt against the Nuri as-Said government and against the British-imposed Hashemite monarchy—a revolt energized by popular dislike of the Baghdad Pact, which ran counter to pan-Arab nationalism, and by popular resentment against even a relatively liberal feudal regime.

Caught by surprise, lacking accurate intelligence, and thoroughly alarmed over losing the last crumbling pillars of Western influence, the American government fell back upon its favorite fallacy—that where there was a revolution it must have been instigated by Moscow and its dupes—in this case, by Moscow and President Nasser. (Actually, Moscow's and Cairo's interests were in conflict.)

And so, much as in China more than a decade earlier, the United States committed the blunder of intervening in a civil conflict with force sufficient to damn the government in power as a puppet of the West, thus assuring its eventual downfall, without intervening in sufficient strength, at the risk of war, to accomplish the objective of sustaining it.

The decision was, of course, reached as "a choice of the lesser evil," the greater evil being to "do nothing and let down our last remaining friends in the Middle East." The rejection of the latter course as "another Munich" rested upon the dubious assumption that Nasser was "another Hitler." Indeed, President Eisenhower all but so described the Egyptian President in his broadcast of July 16.

The fact that Nasser, though an ambitious fanatic, had no military power with which to become a Hitler-like conqueror was ignored, presumably because he was thought to be able to call upon Soviet military power. This supposition completely overlooked President Nasser's outspoken and determined neutralism and the significant fact that he had just spent a week with the arch anti-Soviet neutralist, President Tito of Yugoslavia.

It quickly became evident that the United States and Britain could not count upon the support of majority world opinion. Criticism was rife in the West German press. Austria and Israel formally protested against troops being airlifted across their territory. India's Prime Minister Nehru denounced the landings as "an act of political insanity." At the meeting of the United Nations Security Council the Secretary General's restrained comment left no doubt of his disapproval and dismay. Sweden, Japan, and Panama explicitly voiced their disapproval. The United States and Britain narrowly escaped from having an emergency session of the United Nations General Assembly convened, at Soviet behest, for the express purpose of condemning their action and demanding the immediate withdrawal of their forces.

Even before the Assembly met, it became apparent that, while the Soviet Union could not muster a majority for a resolution demanding condemnation and immediate withdrawal, the United States and Britain would be unable to obtain majority support for any resolution which implied that their intervention had been justified. It was particularly significant that not only the Afro-Asian countries, including Japan, but also the Latin-American delegations were determined that no such implication be conveyed by whatever action the Assembly might take.

Following the lead toward a face-saving exit given by the Secretary General in his opening remarks to the Security Council, President Eisenhower addressed the opening meeting of the Assembly's emergency session with a speech which would have been admirable had it been made six months earlier. The President made it clear that he belatedly recognized the need for coming to terms with Arab nationalism and that the primary responsibility for keeping the peace in the Middle East rested upon the United Nations. Specifically he proposed that a United Nations peace force be established in the Middle East, that the United Nations monitor radio broadcasts and seek to end subversive activity, and that steps be taken to prevent a new spiral of armament. Reversing the previous American stand against regional development bodies, Mr. Eisenhower proposed that a Middle East Development Authority be established and held out the promise of American aid.

The American proposals were coldly received by the Arabs. They accepted the idea of a United Nations-supervised Development Authority but rejected both a United Nations peace force in the Middle East and United Nations monitoring of broadcasts.

President Eisenhower's effort to back up Secretary Dulles in attempting to focus world attention upon the "indirect aggression" of the Moscow-Cairo axis was totally frustrated by the unexpected denouement of the emergency session. The ten Arab states, including Lebanon and Jordan—the original complainants—suddenly united in a resolution which said in effect:

"We have agreed not to interfere with each other. Everyone else please keep out."

The Assembly unanimously accepted the Arab promise, instructing the Secretary General to take such steps as might be necessary to uphold the principles of the United Nations Charter in Lebanon and Jordan. Then the emergency session adjourned.

Thus the unfortunate episode ended with the United States and Britain being provided with the opportunity for a face-saving withdrawal. It remained to be seen whether the Arab states, particularly the United Arab Republic, would live up to the agreement to respect each other's independence and territorial integrity. This seemed not unlikely, at least for a time, since the chief causes for interference had been removed: General Chehab, as the new President of Lebanon, was almost certain to drop his predecessor's pro-Western policy; the pro-Western regime in Iraq had been overthrown; and Jordan's acceptance of the Arab resolution indicated that King Hussein would adopt a conciliatory policy toward the United Arab Republic as the price for continued Jordanian independence.

On the other hand, the future of Arab-Israeli relations remained more than ever uncertain, with a continued truce largely dependent upon the problematical status of Jordan. The crucially important future orientation of Iraq remained unpredictable.

The Western powers—themselves all but thrown out of the Middle East—had obtained no Soviet agreement to refrain from interference in the area, except in so far as such agreement might be implied in Soviet acceptance of the Assembly resolution. Instead of reaching a hands-off agreement with its Soviet adversary, the West had been forced into a one-sided retreat.

As a consequence, the basis for a bargain partially balancing Soviet withdrawal from Eastern Europe by Western withdrawal from the Middle East no longer existed. Neither the precarious British hold on Aden and the Persian Gulf sheikdoms nor the Anglo-American commitments to Israel, Turkey, and Iran could be used as bargaining counters. So far as negotiations with the Kremlin were concerned, what remained of the Western position in the Middle East had become an element of weakness, rather than of strength.

III

There was left the possibility of negotiated disengagement in Europe.

The door to such negotiation remained slightly ajar by reason of the Polish Rapacki Plan for the creation of a nuclear-free zone embracing the two German states, Poland and Czechoslovakia. Although this proposal, when launched in 1957, had aroused considerable interest in Europe, the United States had flatly rejected it early in 1958, chiefly on the grounds that it would tip the balance of military power in favor of the Soviet bloc because it did not provide for the simultaneous withdrawal of foreign conventional forces from the denuclearized zone. This was a valid objection, although the plan as elaborated by Foreign Minister Adam Rapacki envisaged that its adoption would "lead to" conventional disarmament. A Western counterproposal clearly providing for the simultaneous withdrawal of all foreign conventional forces from Germany, Poland, and Czechoslovakia might have been more constructive than an outright flat rejection.

The writer happened to meet Foreign Minister Rapacki during the United Nations Assembly session in August 1958. In a casual conversation he gained the impression that such a counterproposal might still receive serious consideration and that Mr. Rapacki's reason for not having originally included a provision for the withdrawal of foreign conventional forces had been the desire to keep the proposal as simple as possible.

On November 7, 1958, Poland's Deputy Foreign Minister, Josef Winiewicz, announced at a press conference in New York that his government had now added a second stage to its plan —the first stage being a standstill agreement in the nuclear armament of all forces, domestic and foreign, in Czechoslovakia, Poland, and the two German republics. The new second stage, Mr. Winiewicz said, "would be preceded by discussion concerning the adequate reduction of conventional armaments," the agreed-upon reduction of such armaments to be "carried out simultaneously with the complete denuclearization of the zone." The plan proposed that proper provision be made for control measures to enforce both stages.

In response to a request from Mr. Winiewicz for comment upon the revised plan, the writer pointed out that its language was somewhat ambiguous in that it was not clear whether "reduction of conventional armaments" applied to the forces of the four states in the contemplated zone or to foreign troops stationed in the zone, or to both. Mr. Winiewicz replied that the Polish Plan contemplated both.

A few days later the Soviet government launched its political offensive, proposing that West Berlin be created a "free city" while East Berlin would be turned over to the East German "Democratic Republic." The Soviet note gave the Western powers six months to think about and talk about this proposal.

In an article, published in a number of newspapers,[5] the writer made these points:

1. That there could be no solution for Berlin except in the context of a solution for Germany.

2. That there could be no German settlement without recognition that the two widely divergent German states could find their way toward reunification only through a gradual process unhampered by foreign interference.

[5]See *New York Times*, November 24, 1958.

3. That free all-German elections could not be a condition precedent to reunification; that they could come about only as the culmination of a gradual drawing together; and that such a rapprochement between West and East Germany could take place only if both German states first became part of a zone from which foreign coercive power and political domination had been withdrawn.

4. That the Rapacki Plan opened the path to the creation of such a zone, comprising not only the two German states but Poland and Czechoslovakia as well; and that the Western powers would be well advised to take the Polish initiative, rather than the Soviet proposal, as a point of departure.

It was pointed out further that it would be a mistake to think that the Poles were merely fronting for Moscow; that, while both Poles and Russians desired to prevent the nuclear armament of Germany, the Poles had a very definite interest of their own in getting Soviet troops withdrawn from Germany and, eventually, from Poland.

The main point of this article was to emphasize that the Soviet offensive could not be countered merely by denouncing the proposal as to Berlin, and that it was high time for the Western powers to make a proposal of their own, preferably based upon the Rapacki Plan, but in any case putting forward a constructive solution to the German deadlock.

For some years it has been difficult for this observer to understand the strictly negative attitude of the American government toward any and all plans for disengagement in Europe. Ostensibly, the whole of American postwar policy in Europe has been directed toward altering the existing state of affairs in Germany and Eastern Europe. German reunification and the liberation of the Soviet satellites have time and again been proclaimed as the American objectives. Yet whenever the Soviet bloc has indicated an interest in altering the *status quo* in Europe—be it from sincere motivation or merely for propaganda purposes —Washington has backed away, apparently preferring to leave matters as they stood, for fear that any change in the *status quo* would be a change for the worse.

It is impossible to believe that the American government has not realized after all these years that it is absurd to expect the Kremlin to agree to the reunification of Germany merely in order to permit all of Germany, instead of only its western part, to become an armed partner in the anti-Soviet NATO alliance. Yet this is the demand which Washington has made over and over again.

The obvious inference is that Washington, in spite of its avowed aim to reunite Germany and liberate the satellites, actually prefers to leave Germany and Europe divided rather than give up a West German participation in NATO. If this is true, then there is very little hope of negotiating any kind of European settlement.

For those who may be interested in a rebuttal of the more commonly adduced arguments against the military neutralization of Germany, an excerpt from the writer's testimony before the Senate Foreign Relations Committee, on June 4, 1958, is included as supplementary note. (See page 183.)

In view of recent official warnings against "repeating the folly of Versailles" and against "isolating, segregating, neutralizing and demilitarizing" the German people, for fear of making them once more into "a restless, dangerous force,"[6] it is perhaps necessary to define just what such neutralization would and would not mean.

Neutralization means a four-power agreement which, *with German consent*, would provide that a reunified Germany will not enter into any military alliance with either the Western powers or the Soviet bloc. And that is all it means. It would not exclude Germany from a general European security agreement; such an agreement might provide for a limitation of armaments and, perhaps, for the abolition of nuclear weapons; if so, other nations would be subjected to the same limitations. Furthermore, a militarily neutralized Germany would remain completely free to enter into non-military affiliation, such as the European Coal and Steel Community, Euratom and the Common Market. The comparison with the imposed Treaty of Versailles is wholly irrelevant.

[6]See quotations of President Eisenhower and Secretary of State Dulles in the *New York Times* lead editorial of January 28, 1959.

To illustrate the type of counterproposal which, in the writer's opinion, might have been made to the Soviet note of November 27, 1958, there is included in the supplementary notes a draft reply, submitted on December 8, to Secretary Dulles, to the Senate Foreign Relations Committee and to Senate Majority Leader Lyndon Johnson. (See page 186.)

As this book goes to press, no Western initiative has been taken, but there are some indications that Soviet Deputy Premier Mikoyan's unexpected January visit to the United States may have precipitated the long-overdue re-examination of Western policy, at least in Washington and London. If so, a formidable obstacle remains in the person of Chancellor Adenauer. General de Gaulle may prove a second obstacle, since it may well suit the French leader better at this time to support Dr. Adenauer and to keep Germany partitioned, rather than to promote an all-German settlement.

The next few months will determine a fateful question; namely, where—whether in Washington and London or in Bonn and Paris—Western policy is to be formulated. Upon the answer to this question may hang the hope of achieving a European peace settlement.

IV

The task of relaxing tensions in Europe and the Middle East is not hampered by any pretense that the adversary does not exist. Negotiations with Moscow may not be easy or pleasant, but at least the lines of communication are established.

This is not the case in Asia, so far as the United States is concerned. The American government has refused to establish diplomatic relations with the Chinese People's Republic, has kept it out of the United Nations, and has attempted to enforce against it a complete political, economic, and cultural boycott.

The writer has for years urged a revision of this self-defeating policy, contending that it blocks the road to disarmament and to any kind of political settlement in the Far East. Furthermore, he has contended that it divides the anti-communist coalition, alienates the uncommitted peoples, and cements the Sino-

Soviet alliance. As Canada's Lester B. Pearson once remarked: "The head-in-the-sand position is both vulgar and vulnerable."

The four major assumptions upon which American policy has rested are invalid or irrelevant. These are: that the Peking government is illegitimate; that it was imposed upon the Chinese people by outside influence; that it is doomed to fall of its own inner weakness and corruption; and that it is morally "bad."

The Peking government is no more illegitimate than any government which comes to power through successful revolution. Before Mr. Dulles became Secretary of State and accommodated his views to the China Lobby and McCarthyism, he wrote: "If the government of China in fact proves its ability to govern China without serious domestic resistance, then it too should be admitted to the United Nations. Some of the present member nations, and others that might become members, have governments that are not representative of the people. But if in fact they are 'governments'—that is, if they 'govern'—then they have a power which should be represented in any organization which purports to mirror reality."[7]

The Peking government was not imposed or even originally backed by any foreign power. As already pointed out, Stalin was backing Chiang Kai-shek when the civil war began and switched his support to the communists only after they had destroyed the flower of the Nationalist armies. Until that time, Mao Tse-tung received less support from Russia than Chiang Kai-shek obtained from the United States.

As for internal weakness, the Peking regime is, by all competent accounts, the least corrupt and the most efficient, even if coercive, government that Chinese now living can remember. The available evidence indicates that the vast majority of the Chinese people consider themselves better off, and certainly no worse off, than they were under the inefficient and equally coercive Kuomintang. It is doubtful that many mainland

[7]John Foster Dulles, *War or Peace*. The quotation appears both in the original edition, published in 1950, and in the revised edition, published in 1957.

Chinese would agree with Mr. Dulles that their government is weak and likely to be overthrown.

Nor would many Chinese agree with Mr. Dulles that their government is a morally "bad" government. Moreover, in 1950 Mr. Dulles himself wrote:

"All nations should be members [of the United Nations] without attempting to appraise closely those which are 'good' and those which are 'bad.' Already that distinction is obliterated by the present membership of the United Nations."[8]

Yet in the same year in which a second edition of his book appeared—on July 15, 1957—Mr. Dulles, in a speech at San Francisco, justified keeping the People's Republic of China out of the United Nations on the grounds that the United Nations was not "a reformatory for 'bad' governments." The United Nations was, he said, "an association of peace-loving states, devoted to their obligations under the Charter." (And this less than a year after one member's tanks had rolled into Budapest and the armed forces of three other members had invaded Egypt!)

President Eisenhower, too, catered to emotion. On one occasion, when asked about relaxing trade restrictions, he replied that he did not think the American people wanted to have anything to do with a regime "whose hands are dripping with the blood of American soldiers." (What former enemy's hands have not dripped with American blood? What about Germany? What about Japan?)

During the Middle East crisis of 1958—and especially after Premier Khrushchev's visit to Peking—the feeling grew among thoughtful Americans in and out of Congress that it was time to get off the brink of war with China, to recognize the existing facts, and to prevent another crisis from erupting in the Far East. To counter this rapidly growing sentiment, the State Department released on August 9 a long directive to its embassies abroad, reaffirming all the old arguments, including the contention that continued non-recognition by the United States would strengthen the likelihood that the Peking regime would be overthrown.

[8]Ibid.

By whom? By Chiang Kai-shek?

The United States had solemnly agreed in 1943 that Formosa (Taiwan) and the Pescadores "should be returned to the Republic of China." The Cairo Declaration did not say: "to a friendly Republic of China." When Japan surrendered and eventually signed a peace treaty (in 1952) it renounced "all rights, title and claim to Formosa" without mention of China as the beneficiary. (This was because of Anglo-American disagreement as to which Chinese regime had the better claim.) Thus Taiwan was surrendered to the forty-eight signatories of the peace treaty, not one of which thereby acquired a legal title.

Long before the peace treaty, in 1945, the Nationalist regime declared that Taiwan had become the thirty-fifth province of China. The Nationalists occupied the island by force, killing several thousand Formosans who objected. Neither then nor later have the wishes of the eight million Formosans been considered.

The Nationalist title to Taiwan rests either upon the pretense that Chiang Kai-shek is still China's legitimate ruler or upon the theory that Taiwan has become a separate state. The latter theory is repudiated by the Nationalists.

Three days after Chiang Kai-shek fled the mainland, the United States reaffirmed (October 4, 1949) recognition of the Nationalist regime as the legitimate government of China. But, prior to the Korean War, neither the Truman administration nor the American Chiefs of Staff entertained the notion that Taiwan was a base essential to the defense of the United States and the "free world" position in Asia. In fact, on January 5, 1950, President Truman declared:

> The United States government will not pursue a course which leads to involvement in civil conflict in China. Similarly, the United States government will not provide military aid or advice to Chinese forces on Formosa.

During the Korean War, President Truman was anxious to keep the conflict from spreading. He refused Chiang's offer of Nationalist troops and ordered the United States Seventh Fleet to prevent both Communist attack upon Taiwan and

Nationalist attack upon the mainland, thus neutralizing the Nationalists.

Upon his accession to office, President Eisenhower reversed this policy, "unleashing" Chiang Kai-shek and stating that the United States Seventh Fleet would no longer be "employed to shield Communist China."

In the writer's opinion, this was a serious and far-reaching mistake. Having stopped the fighting in Korea on terms which would have been angrily repudiated by an inflamed American public if President Truman had accepted them a few months earlier, President Eisenhower was in a position to disentangle the United States from its involvement in the Nationalist-Communist struggle for control of China. Whatever moral obligation the United States owed Chiang Kai-shek as an ally in the war against Japan had been more than fulfilled. The Nationalist leader was certainly entitled to asylum if he did not wish to make peace with history and return to his country; he was not, in this observer's opinion, entitled to keep the United States entangled in the web of his forlorn hopes for a reconquest of the mainland, nor to remain himself a constant provocation to a war which might well engulf all humanity.

Whatever may be said for the Eisenhower administration's contrary view, there was certainly no moral, legal, or common-sense justification for the policy it pursued with respect to the Nationalist-held Chinese offshore islands. Twice—in 1954–55 and again in 1958—Secretary Dulles took the United States to the brink of war over these small islands which had nothing whatever to do with the legal status of Taiwan and were in no way essential to its defense. Instead of urging their quiet evacuation, Mr. Dulles—as part of the policy of "unleashing Chiang Kai-shek"—permitted, if he did not actually encourage, the Generalissimo to fortify the islands and to use them as offensive bases against the mainland. Since the Nationalist leader scarcely concealed his desire to get the United States into war with the Peking regime, nothing suited him better than to stake his waning prestige upon holding the Tachen, Matsu, and Quemoy islands under the guns of hostile shore-based artillery, gambling on the chance that the United States would intervene if the islands were seriously attacked.

The first crisis resulting from this provocative action arose in 1954–55, when the Chinese Communists attacked the Tachen Islands. On this occasion President Eisenhower refused to be stampeded into committing the United States to the defense of the offshore islands, asking Congress to pass a resolution leaving it up to him to decide whether any eventual attack upon the offshore islands was to be construed as an attack upon Taiwan. Congress passed the resolution with only three dissenting votes in the House and three in the Senate.

Subsequently the Nationalists were persuaded, in exchange for a formal mutual-defense treaty, to withdraw their Tachen garrison, the evacuation being accomplished with American help and without interference from the mainland. Tension then subsided for a period of three years until the Middle East crisis of 1958 brought Premier Khrushchev to Peking.

Instead of using the three-year interval of calm to persuade Chiang Kai-shek to evacuate or thin out his garrisons on the other offshore islands, the United States permitted the Nationalists to reinforce and fortify Matsu and Quemoy and to continue using these islands to block the Fukien ports of Foochow and Amoy.

The second crisis began on August 23, 1958, with a sustained Communist artillery bombardment of Quemoy. This was undoubtedly part of the Sino-Soviet strategy planned at Peking. Within a week it appeared likely that, unless the United States intervened, the island would be starved into surrender. Surrender would mean that the Nationalists would lose about one third of their defense force. Having permitted the foolish commitment of these troops to the defense of Quemoy, Mr. Dulles now succeeded in convincing the President that, because of their presence on Quemoy, the loss of the island would endanger the defense of Taiwan as well as strike a fatal blow at the prestige of the Nationalist regime.

Thus, for the second time, Mr. Dulles took the United States to the brink of a war which would almost certainly bring the

125

Soviet Union to China's defense, while leaving the United States without willing allies or even sympathizers.

This time President Eisenhower went along with his Secretary of State, conveying the distinct impression that, if necessary, he would take the nation to war in order to prevent Quemoy from falling to the Communists.

Many Americans were deeply shocked by the President's acquiescence in the reckless maneuvers of his Secretary of State. Among others, the writer sent the following letter, dated September 3, 1958, to the New York *Times* and to a number of leading newspapers across the country.

It is almost inconceivable that, with our troops still in Lebanon, we should find ourselves for the second time at the brink of war with China over two little groups of offshore islands—which—whatever the status of Taiwan—clearly belong to the mainland.

It is equally incredible that the vacillation, blundering and sudden irresponsible actions of our government, which constitute a threat to all humanity, should have aroused practically no protest from the American people.

As to this latest venture in brinkmanship, American military authorities have never considered Matsu and Quemoy vital to the defense of Taiwan, any more than the Tachen Islands evacuated during the previous crisis. Matsu and Quemoy became important only because, as part of the policy of "unleashing Chiang Kai-shek," the United States urged the Generalissimo to fortify the islands as offensive outposts. If, as President Eisenhower has said, these islands are now more important than they were, it is because— at our own urging—Chiang Kai-shek has committed one-third of his forces and what remains of his prestige to their defense.

The only sensible answer is to help evacuate these forces as quickly as possible.

Let us suppose that, after Cornwallis' surrender, the British had refused to recognize the finality of their defeat and, expressing their determination to return to the mainland, had withdrawn most of their forces to an imaginary island lying 100 miles off our Middle Atlantic coast. Let us suppose further that the Royal Navy and a few of King George's redcoats had clung to Nantucket, Long Island and the Florida Keys, using these offshore islands as bases from which to interfere with American shipping and to launch occasional raids upon the mainland.

How long would the Founding Fathers have tolerated such a situation?

And how would the American people have felt toward France, if, instead of aiding the American Revolution, Louis XVI and his foreign minister Vergennes had decided to back the British, had refused to accept their defeat and had sent Rochambeau's fleet to help the British defend their remaining island strongholds? (Incidentally, according to the Dulles doctrine, French assistance to the American rebellion would have been adjudged as "indirect aggression.")

How mopic with respect to our own real interests and how ruthlessly inconsiderate of the interests of humanity are we going to allow our government to be? How long shall we be silent, while our government recklessly takes us from one brink to another? Is there no "loyal opposition" which, instead of acquiescing in, if not actually applauding, each act of insanity, will at long last demand an end to irresponsibility and propose some common-sense alternatives?

This is a time when true patriotism demands not quiet acquiescence but loud protest.

If we get into a major war over Matsu and Quemoy, we shall have few friends and allies; nor shall we deserve them. We shall have no one to blame but ourselves, nothing to gain and everything to lose—including our self-respect and our national honor.

If Mr. Dulles has made or implied rash promises to Chiang Kai-shek, unauthorized by the President, it is his honor—not ours—that may be at stake in a reversal of policy.

Even if a last-minute return to sanity were to involve the repudiation of a promise given by the President, the American people have a right to repudiate the promise. Their own honor and "a decent respect to the opinions of mankind" would permit no other action. Who are we to decide for all humanity that the risk of extinction is preferable to letting the Chinese Communists take over two little groups of islands to which we ourselves have not the shadow of legal or moral right?

This letter was quickly followed by statements from a considerable number of others, including former Air Force Secretary Thomas K. Finletter, former Secretary of State Dean Acheson, former Senator Herbert H. Lehman, and the then chairman of the Senate Foreign Relations Committee, Senator Theodore Green of Rhode Island.

Perhaps because his was the first citizen protest to appear in print, the writer received a flood of concurring letters, telegrams, and long-distance telephone calls originating from Maine to California. Most of these messages could be summarized as saying: "You have exactly expressed our feelings. Tell us what we can do."

In response to this demand, the writer drafted an appeal to the President, asking him to call an immediate session of Congress, the text of which may be found among the supplementary notes to this chapter (See page 190.) This appeal was inserted in the *New York Times* as a paid half-page advertisement. A coupon signed by the writer suggested that those who agreed might do three things: (1) Sign the petition and send it to the President, to their two Senators, and to their Congressman. (2) Form a group to run the petition in their local newspapers. (3) Make whatever financial contribution they might wish to the further dissemination of the petition.

Within a week, thousands of petitions went to the White House, some with as many as 150 signatures. In a number of cities the advertisement was run by local groups. Financial contributions, ranging from one dollar upward were received in an amount very nearly equaling the $2,700 cost of the original advertisement.

Hundreds of people wrote to say that they had written personal letters to the President or to their representatives in Congress. Several Senators and Representatives issued their own call for convening the Congress or, at the very least, the legislative leaders.

Quite obviously, there had been widespread latent opposition to the administration's China policy. It had required only a spark to ignite it. In answer to a reporter's question, the State Department said that its mail was running 80 per cent against going to war over Quemoy.

Vice-President Nixon promptly denounced the State Department official who gave out this information as "sabotaging" the policy of his chief. This injudicious outburst, plus the President's own references to "misguided people" who were criticizing his policy, served merely to arouse further criticism.

By the last week of September, behind-the-scenes pressure from Britain, Norway, and other NATO countries, plus public pressure from the American people, had mounted to a point where the administration felt itself compelled to modify its policy. At his press conference of September 30, an obviously embarrassed Secretary of State recognized publicly for the first time that Chiang Kai-shek could never reconquer the mainland; that the United States would not aid any attempt to do so; that Chiang's only chance to return to the mainland would be if the Peking regime were overthrown by revolution; and that even in that event Chiang's chances of being called back would be slim. Furthermore, Mr. Dulles now characterized as "foolish" the action of the Generalissimo in stationing so large a part of his forces on the offshore islands, clearly implying that he was seeking a way to bring about their withdrawal without hopelessly damaging Nationalist prestige.

The next day President Eisenhower echoed the same changed attitude. Forgotten were his previous statements that the loss of Quemoy would endanger Taiwan and threaten to topple the whole "free-world position" in the Western Pacific. Forgotten, too, was the President's earlier contention that a withdrawal from Quemoy would constitute "another Munich."

In spite of this apparent partial reversal of policy, the situation with respect to the offshore islands remained substantially unaltered. The ambiguous communiqué issued after Secretary Dulles' visit to Taiwan in October by no means guaranteed that the Generalissimo had renounced the use of force against the mainland, even though it sought to convey that impression. As for Peking, it seemed evident that Mao Tse-tung's objective was not to obtain a Nationalist withdrawal from Matsu and Quemoy but, rather, to keep the pot boiling and to avoid separating the question of the offshore islands from the question of Taiwan itself. No other hypothesis seemed to explain the cynical, almost humorous (and typically Chinese) alternate-day bombardment of Quemoy which began after Mr. Dulles' departure from Taipei.

It became apparent that, so long as this state of affairs might continue, the United States—and, with it, the entire human race—would remain at the edge of an abyss into which it could at any moment be plunged by the rash act of either side in the Chinese civil conflict. For, while few of America's allies were prepared to fight for Quemoy, it remained a fact that if the United States were to become embroiled in a war with China, and if the Soviet Union were to come to China's assistance, the entire world would inevitably become involved. Hence the quiet but persistent pressure upon Washington from both friendly and "neutral" nations for a modification of American policy.

In the opinion of this observer, the required modification of American policy affects far more than Washington's stand concerning the offshore islands; it goes to the root of our whole China policy.

Late in 1958 it became fairly obvious that Mr. Dulles was prepared to sacrifice or force Chiang Kai-shek to sacrifice the offshore islands if, in exchange, he could get both Peking and Taipei to accept what has been called a "two-China policy"— meaning the renunciation by Chiang Kai-shek of his hope of returning to the mainland and the renunciation by Peking of its claim to Taiwan. However, the idea of "two Chinas" was indignantly rejected by both Chiang and Mao, each insisting that the civil war must be fought or otherwise brought to a conclusion by total victory.

It became equally obvious that America's allies—and world opinion in general—would support a defense of Taiwan against Communist attack, if the question of the offshore islands were eliminated. This was perhaps partly because, in the existing circumstances, such an attack seemed unlikely, but even more because of the sharp distinction between what world opinion considered to be the legal and moral status of Taiwan as against what it held to be the legal and moral status of the offshore islands.

The problem, then, was one of eliminating or mitigating the danger of war by means which would command the allegiance and support of world opinion.

To this problem there was and is no sure or easy answer. No one can tell whether the Sino-Soviet axis would accept *any* settlement at the present time, even a settlement endorsed as fair by an overwhelming majority of world opinion.

There is, however, the possibility of envisaging what shape such a settlement might take and what modifications in American policy it would entail. The following are the major points upon which the writer believes that an American offer might be based:

1. In exchange for Peking's agreement to permit the evacuation of the offshore island garrisons and such of the local populations as might wish to be evacuated, the United States would recognize Peking's claim to the islands, subject to final determination by the International Court of Justice.

2. The United States would withdraw its objection to admitting the People's Republic of China to the United Nations upon the following prior conditions:

(a) That Peking shall have agreed to permit the people of Taiwan and the Pescadores to decide their own destiny after a period of five years, during which these islands would be militarily neutralized under United Nations or other neutral supervision. Such neutralization would involve the demilitarization of Taiwan and the Pescadores except for such military, naval, and air forces as might be furnished for their protection by or at the request of the United Nations or other supervising authority.

(b) That the People's Republic of China and the Soviet Union shall have agreed to the reunification of Korea and Vietnam under free elections conducted under United Nations or other neutral supervision; and that China, the Soviet Union, and the United States shall have agreed not to interfere in any way in the internal affairs of these two countries, channeling whatever economic aid they may thereafter wish to provide through the United Nations.

(c) That the People's Republic of China shall have released all unjustifiably held American prisoners.

(d) That the People's Republic of China shall agree to accept the obligations embodied in the United Nations Charter and to co-operate with the United Nations in bringing the nuclear arms race to a halt and in working toward universal national disarmament.

3. In addition to offering the People's Republic of China membership in the United Nations upon these terms, the writer would suggest that the United States should, in its own interest, offer to establish diplomatic relations, to permit mutual free access to newsmen, businessmen, students, and cultural visitors and to remove restrictions upon trade except as to arms and materials directly relevant to arms manufacture.

Were these or similar terms to be offered to Peking and accepted, the danger of war in the Far East would be all but eliminated. If these terms were offered by the United States and rejected, majority world opinion, including majority opinion in the crucially important uncommitted nations, would, in this observer's opinion, swing to the support of the United States.

As said earlier, there can be no guarantee that a revised American policy will bring peace to the Far East. All that can be said with certainty is that our present China policy keeps the world at the brink of war, forecloses all chance of peaceable settlement, divides the anti-communist coalition, alienates the uncommitted peoples, and cements the Sino-Soviet alliance.

V

The crises of 1958 undoubtedly awakened a large part of the American people to a realization of the need for a drastic revision of the whole of United States foreign policy. The fall of the Fourth French Republic over the Algerian crisis provided dramatic proof that anti-colonial revolt could no longer be suppressed by military force. The renewed Soviet threat to Berlin reawakened awareness of the danger lurking in the continued deadlock over Germany. The Middle East debacle established the futility of Western policy in that area. The Quemoy crisis exploded the myth upon which American policy in the Far East had been based and, for the first time, brought debate over that policy out into the open. Above all, two uncomfortably narrow escapes from war had shaken the confidence of many Americans in the competence and common sense of their government. This was clearly reflected in the November elections.

What remained uncertain was the extent to which the Eisenhower administration had learned from the bitter experiences of 1958, and the extent to which it might be helped or hindered in revitalizing its obsolete foreign policy by a victory-flushed Democratic opposition in unchallengeable control of both Houses of Congress.

We have been concerned, in this chapter, with the possibilities of reducing critical tensions between the two rival power orbits by negotiation leading to disengagement and disarmament. Somewhat removed from the areas of direct confrontation and potential conflict, two other crises were brewing during 1958—one in Japan and the other in India. These two countries are the twin hinges upon which will swing the future of non-communist Asia. Since their problems are not matters to be settled by negotiation with the communist dictatorships but, rather, questions to be confronted within the non-communist orbit, they will be discussed in the context of Anglo-American co-operation.

CHAPTER NINE

The Anglo-American Alliance

With the kaleidoscopic changes taking place in many parts of the world and with the post-de Gaulle future of France as unpredictable as the post-Adenauer future of Germany, Great Britain and the United States are more than ever important both to each other and as the nerve and brain centers of the Western community. Canada is playing an increasingly vital role as a halfway house in the Anglo-American alliance. Upon the close co-ordination of the foreign policy of these three nations will hang much of the future of the Western community.

Taking the postwar period as a whole, Anglo-American coordination of policy has been most effective in Europe and least effective in Asia, especially in the Far East.

With respect to China, there has been an open divergence of policy. Neither Britain nor Canada has associated itself with American involvement in the Chinese civil war, especially not with the American alliance with the Nationalist regime after its flight to Taiwan. Both Britain and Canada supported American action in halting North Korean aggression but vainly tried to exercise a restraining influence upon carrying the war into North Korea. In the crises of 1955 and 1958 over the offshore islands, both the British and Canadian governments counseled caution. Until American policy with respect to China undergoes a radical change along lines indicated in the preceding chapter, the Far East will remain a dangerous source of Anglo-American disunity.

Apart from disagreement over Chinese policy, there has been too little Anglo-American co-operation in dealing with Japan and India.

Britain has long felt a natural sympathy for Japan, partly because of Japan's former function as a barrier to Russian expansion but probably even more because Japan's economic position so closely resembles that of the United Kingdom. Both are island nations dependent upon overseas trade for their existence.

On the other hand, Australia, New Zealand, and the Philippines share with the United States an attitude still largely influenced both by the recent war and by economic interests hostile to Japan as a trade competitor.

The future orientation of Japan is crucially important to the entire Western community. At present Japan stands in a position of isolation. She is separated from Asia in part by her own predatory past and in part by the cold-war restrictions imposed by the United States. Her 91 million people live in an area smaller than California—an area only 16 per cent of which is arable. They comprise the most literate and highly skilled labor force in Asia. Japan's only assets are ample rainfall and highly developed industry. From the strategic point of view, Japan is the one effective logistical base and repair shop in Asia.

At present Japan depends for her security upon the United States under the 1952 peace treaty, now under badly needed revision. From an economic point of view, Japan is heavily dependent upon access to the American market; at present she buys roughly twice as much from the United States as she is permitted to sell in the American market. She is the second largest importer of American goods. Japanese purchases in the United States total over $1.2 billion per annum, of which about $500 million consist of agricultural produce.

It is inevitable that Japan will eventually go where she can earn a living. A restrictive policy, especially on the part of the United States, will drive the Japanese into accommodation with the communist orbit. Recognizing legitimate American fear of excessive competition, Japan has imposed voluntary export quotas and taken measures to halt the pirating of Western designs. (Incidentally, much of the Japanese pirating in the past has been encouraged by American importers.) Unless the defense treaty is revised so as to become an agreement between equals, instead of an imposed settlement, and unless Japan's economic needs are given serious consideration by the West—in terms of trade opportunities rather than aid—Japan will be driven into playing off one side in the cold war against the other—if, indeed, she is not driven altogether into the communist orbit.

So long as the cold war continues, Japan is very nearly as important to the West as Western Europe. If Japan is lost to the Western trading community, most of Southeast Asia will inevitably follow in her footsteps.

Because of Britain's natural understanding of the Japanese dilemma and because Britain does not share the onus of having conquered, destroyed, and occupied Japan, Washington would be well advised to draw heavily upon British co-operation in developing future policy.

For different reasons, closer Anglo-American consultation is desirable with respect to India. Where Japan is crucially important as Asia's most highly developed industrial complex, India is even more important in political and psychological terms. India is where democracy in Asia will succeed or fail. The United States possesses the economic resources required to give India the help she needs, but Britain possesses a far greater understanding of India and of the Indian people and —because of her graceful withdrawal—a considerable reservoir of good will.

India's greatest difficulty in meeting the demands of the Revolution of Rising Expectations is her inadequate food production and her inability to derive from her agriculture the capital needed for industrialization and economic progress. With a population which will soon reach 400 million chiefly engaged in agriculture, India produces only about 68 million tons of food grain per annum, while China's 600 million people produce 185 million tons. Each year there are about 5 million new mouths to feed.

Per capita income in India is about $56 per year. Over 60 per cent of India's total consumer spending goes for food. Among the millions of landless peasants, the figure amounts to 85 per cent.

The worst of it is that, as part of India's impoverished masses are brought into employment, their increased ability to buy food has caused food prices to rise at a fantastic rate. From June 1955 to May 1957 the price of rice rose almost 70 per cent, wheat rose 54 per cent, and the two coarse grains which form the staple diet of the poor rose by 96.5 per cent and 196.8 per cent.

The crux of India's problem is how to produce more food and how to derive at least some capital from increased agricultural production.

The United States could materially assist India in meeting this part of her problem by a method which would also benefit the American farmers. Instead of accumulating and eventually destroying or dumping the huge grain surpluses created by price supports, the United States could deliberately encourage the growing of special food grains for Indian consumption. These grains would be bought from American farmers at fair prices by the American government and would then be given to India in the form of outright grants. This would enable the Indian government to arrest inflation, control prices, and use the proceeds of sale for economic development. In other words, the United States—and also Canada and Australia—could use their surplus agricultural capacity to raise food which could be used *as capital* to promote the economic development of food-deficit countries.

A second major obstacle to the success of India's five-year plan has been the increased military expenditure which the Indian government has had to incur as the result of American rearming of Pakistan. In the writer's opinion, rearming Pakistan was a serious mistake which it is not too late even now to remedy. Military aid to Pakistan has not only adversely affected India but has turned Afghanistan toward the Soviet Union.

It is difficult to see how anyone could have thought that these clearly predictable consequences would be more than offset by attempting to make a useful military ally out of an artificially created, theocratic state whose western and eastern parts not only have little in common but are separated from each other by one thousand miles of democratic and pacifist India. British influence could be extremely helpful in revising both the SEATO and Baghdad alliances and in making it possible for the United States to convert military aid to Pakistan into much-needed economic assistance.

Finally, the Indian five-year plan is in trouble because India lacks foreign exchange to pay not only for food imports but for some of the capital equipment required by the development plan.

These were the major reasons why India applied to the Western countries in 1957 for aid amounting to $1.2 billion, of which she hoped to obtain about half from the United States.

It was not until after the Middle East debacle of July–August 1958 and the renewed outbreak of hostilities over the Chinese offshore islands that the Western powers took a serious view of the Indian crisis. On August 26, 1958, it was announced that, on British initiative, the World Bank had taken the lead in arranging for loans totaling $350 million, of which the World Bank, Britain, and the American Development Loan Fund would each provide $100 million, Germany $40 million, and Japan $10 million, with Canada perhaps adding an outright grant or loan of $17 million. In addition, the United States undertook to sell India $200 million worth of surplus food for rupees. These funds will presumably cover India's needs until March 1959, but another $600 million at least will be required after that date to see the five-year plan through to completion.

Prior to August 1958, the response of the American government to India's requests for aid had been not only wholly inadequate but almost incredibly dilatory. This was more the fault of the administration than of Congress, even though the 85th Congress was notoriously reluctant to support even the timid foreign aid programs put forward by President Eisenhower.

Reviewing the postwar history of Western policy in Asia, one might say that, had Britain been able to exert a stronger influence upon American policy, the result might have been considerably better both for Asia and for the West. Britain has suffered not from a lack of experience and understanding nor from inability to formulate a constructive Asian policy but from a lack of self-confidence and economic power. The United States, on the other hand, has suffered—to put it crudely—from possessing more brawn than brains or experience. The combination would have worked more effectively if each partner had more clearly recognized his own deficiency and the other's potential strength.

When we come to the Middle East, we find an entirely different relation between the two partners, a relationship in which the United States allowed itself to fall heir to an unwise and obsolete British policy.

Britain originally became interested in the Middle East primarily in order to secure her life line to India. Hence her original presence in Egypt, her colony at Aden, and her protectorate over the Persian Gulf sheikdoms. The discovery of oil in Iran and Mosul, just prior to World War I, gave the area a wholly new importance.

As the reward for Arab co-operation in fighting the Turks in World War I, the British promised the Arabs independence, presumably under the Hashemite dynasty. Instead, the Arab lands—except for Saudi Arabia and Yemen—were cynically divided into British and French spheres of influence, each composed of a number of artificially created states, nominally independent but actually dominated by the two Western powers mostly under League of Nations mandates. The French were forced out of Syria and Lebanon during the course of World War II. Most of the nominally independent regimes established by the British were feudal, corrupt, and oppressive.

The fact is that when Britain came into control of the Arab Middle East she was already past her prime as an imperial power. In contrast to the long years of responsible governance in India, of building improvements, training troops and administrators, and of close Anglo-Indian personal association, no such tradition grew up between Britain and the Arab peoples. Britain came into the Middle East as a policeman to keep others out. After the discovery of oil, she became an exploiter of Arab resources without establishing any close relationship with the Arab peoples, her chief interest being in the establishment or preservation of governments willing to grant concessions and to accept British direction of their foreign relations.

Before the discovery of oil, the American interest in the Middle East had been almost entirely cultural. When American oil companies entered the field, American policy began to fall into the pattern set by the British. As British military and economic power waned during and after World War II, the United States became the dominant factor in the area, in one sense competing with Britain and, in another, taking over British responsibility and British policy.

Whereas Britain's retreat from India was accomplished without leaving more than a minimum of resentment, her retreat from the Middle East became a stubbornly contested withdrawal, leaving behind a maximum of hostility. To this hostility the United States fell heir because it developed no policy of its own, shaping its improvised course solely with an eye to the cold war, the creation of Israel, and the exploitation of Middle Eastern petroleum resources.

The author has elsewhere dealt at length with the historical background of the mid-century Middle East crisis which began with the creation of Israel.[1] It is intended here only to review briefly those Anglo-American actions in the postwar period which have directly contributed to the critical situation which arose in 1958.

When the British gave up their mandate over Palestine, President Truman acted somewhat impulsively in sponsoring the 1947 partition resolution in the United Nations, without recognizing that the creation of Israel (instead of a bi-national Jewish-Arab state) directly conflicted both with his desire to make anti-communist military allies of the Arab states and with the Anglo-American desire to retain monopolistic control of

[1]Op. cit., *Agenda for Action.*

Arabian oil. Had he faced the choice and opted for the creation of Israel, abandoning the notion of arming the Arab states against Russia, much of the subsequent trouble would have been avoided.

When the Arab states attacked Israel and were defeated, the United States failed to support the United Nations in backing up the original terms of the partition resolution. This created additional problems and greatly increased the number of Arab refugees.

On October 13, 1951, the United States, Britain, France, and Turkey presented to King Farouk a proposal for a Middle East anti-communist alliance. Farouk declined, realizing that the proposed treaty would perpetuate the British presence in Suez.

Rebuffed by Egypt, the Western powers nevertheless laid their plan before the other Arab states. This produced a political crisis in Syria, where Colonel Shishekly took over as dictator on November 29, 1951. Shishekly, although pro-Western, declined to become involved in the cold war, thus emphasizing the determination of even pro-Western Arab leaders to maintain a policy of non-alignment. This might have ended the matter had it not been for the advent of John Foster Dulles as Secretary of State.

Mr. Dulles visited the Middle East in the spring of 1953. Hinting strongly that the pro-Israel policy of the United States was now a thing of the past, the Secretary of State called upon General Naguib, the new ruler of Egypt, and in the name of President Eisenhower presented him with the symbolic gift of a pistol. Egypt was promised help in persuading the British to agree to an earlier evacuation of the Suez base than was provided for in the Anglo-Egyptian Treaty of 1936. On July 15, 1954, President Eisenhower declared that the United States would enter into "firm commitments" with regard to military and economic assistance if Prime Minister Nasser, soon to become President, were to arrive at a satisfactory settlement with the British. When the British did agree in the autumn of 1954 to withdraw from Suez, the American government openly expressed its gratification. Nasser was hailed in the American press as "a thoroughly dedicated and undictatorial ruler."

It appeared that by taking Egypt's side against Britain and the Arab side against Israel, Mr. Dulles might be developing a new American policy which, whatever else one might think of it, would at least have the virtue of consistency. However, appearances were deceptive.

Even while he was helping Nasser to become independent of Britain, Mr. Dulles was preparing a move which, whether or not he realized it, would be a shocking blow to Egyptian ambitions. At Baghdad on February 24, 1955, Turkey and Iraq, urged on by Mr. Dulles, signed a pact of "mutual co-operation," soon to be extended to include Britain and, later, Iran and Pakistan. Iraq was Egypt's rival for leadership among the Arab states, and the Iraqi government was considered in Cairo to be little more than a British puppet. With Britain herself joining the Baghdad Pact, the whole matter could not fail to appear to the Arabs as an anti-Egyptian maneuver, inspired by annoyance at Nasser's continued refusal to co-operate in forming a Middle East Defense Organization and by the desire to perpetuate Western control of the Middle East.

The consequences were immediate and far-reaching. A storm of resentment broke throughout the Arab world, except in Iraq, where Nasser's bitterest enemy, Nuri as-Said, suppressed all expression of discontent.

Jordan, Britain's creation and closest Middle Eastern ally, refused to sign the alliance.

The most serious consequence of the Baghdad Pact was, of course, that Nasser turned to Moscow for arms in order to offset the Western arming of Iraq. The United States could have provided Egypt with arms, but here, with curious inconsistency, the American government suddenly remembered its obligations to Israel and feared that Nasser would use any armaments furnished him to attack the Jewish state. As a result of this almost incredible vacillation between a pro-Egyptian and an anti-Egyptian policy, the American and British governments opened the door to Soviet penetration of an area which British power had for over a century defended against Russian encroachment. But this was not all.

During the honeymoon with Nasser, the United States, the

American-controlled World Bank, and Great Britain had made an offer to Egypt to finance the Aswan High Dam. On July 10, 1956, Mr. Dulles suddenly withdrew the American offer in order to punish Nasser for having bought arms from Russia and for having recognized the People's Republic of China. The reasons given, in extraordinarily undiplomatic language, were that Egypt had failed to reach an agreement with the Sudan concerning the use of the Nile waters and that the Egyptian economy had been prejudiced by pledging a part of the cotton crop to the Soviet Union in payment for the arms received. (There had been no water-sharing agreement with the Sudan when the offer was made and there was nothing particularly new about Egypt's bartering its cotton crop for needed imports.)

According to Mr. Dulles' authorized biographer, Jack Beal of the *Time-Life* organization, this was "a deliberate gambit" undertaken by the Secretary of State. If so, it is a strange fact that, according to a reputable reporter, there was not in the State Department a single position paper analyzing the gambit's probable effect.[2] When Nasser retaliated by nationalizing the Suez Canal on July 26, 1956, the American government was taken completely by surprise.

The facts concerning the Franco-British reaction to the seizure of the canal are too fresh in memory to require repetition here. It need only be recalled that the morally and legally correct position taken by the American government in condemning the Anglo-French-Israeli invasion of Egypt was stultified by the fact that the United States had not only itself provoked the Suez crisis but that the American government had for years closed its eyes to Egyptian raids against Israel, to the illegal Egyptian blockade of Israeli shipping, and to Egyptian preparation for a "second round" attempt to drive the Israelis into the sea.

The net result of the Suez fiasco was that Nasser was saved from a second defeat in a preventive Israeli war which he had himself provoked; that what remained of Anglo-French prestige

[2]See C. L. Sulzberger in the *New York Times* of April 7, 1957.

in the Arab world was destroyed; and that the United States found itself in the embarrassing position of having taken sides with the Soviet Union against its oldest allies.

Having worked the United States into this unhappy predicament, the Eisenhower administration seemed for a short time to have surrendered the Middle East problem to the United Nations. Soon, however, Mr. Dulles again undertook unilateral action. The "Eisenhower Doctrine" of January 1957 promised American armed intervention on behalf of any Middle Eastern state which might find itself the victim of overt aggression by "any nation controlled by international communism." No Middle Eastern state had asked for any such guarantee. Obsessed with military thinking, the United States attempted to lock the door against a danger which scarcely existed, ignoring the much more real danger of indigenous revolution fostered by external and not necessarily communist influence.

Only one Arab government, the Chamoun government of Lebanon, accepted the Eisenhower Doctrine and thereby signed its own death warrant. Jordan, Saudi Arabia, and even Iraq declined.

Nevertheless, when revolutionary elements appeared likely to overthrow the Hashemite monarchy in Jordan, President Eisenhower ordered the Sixth Fleet into the Eastern Mediterranean. This bit of "gunboat diplomacy"—a preview of what was to happen a year later—merely served to identify King Hussein even more clearly in Arab eyes as a protégé of the West.

Faced by continued threats of revolution in Jordan openly encouraged by Cairo, and by leftist rumbling in Syria apparently encouraged by Moscow, Mr. Dulles now attempted to salvage the rapidly deteriorating Western position by backing King Saud, the most reactionary of all Arab potentates, as a counter-force to Nasserism and communism. The King's utter failure as a mediator in the Jordanian and Turkish-Syrian crises of 1957 led to his being forced to surrender most of his power to his neutralist-minded brother Faisal. Except for tiny Lebanon, this left the United States with only one ally in the Arab world; namely, the Nuri as-Said government of Iraq.

Having engineered the disastrous Baghdad alliance, the

United States had originally been unwilling to join it for fear of alienating Nasser. But, having thoroughly alienated Nasser, the United States, in 1957 and the first half of 1958, still refused repeated Turkish, Iraqi, and Iranian urgings to give the alliance full support. This was probably the final straw which toppled the Nuri as-Said regime. (Characteristically, when the Iraqi government had fallen and the alliance lay in ruins, Mr. Dulles hastened to enter into "full partnership" by an Executive agreement which avoided the necessity of obtaining the consent of the Senate.)

Meanwhile, American troops had been landed in Lebanon, British troops had parachuted into Jordan, and the United States Ambassador to the United Nations had denounced the new Iraqi government as a gang of murderers. Yet, as soon as it became clear that the new Iraqi government was firmly established and apparently had no intention of joining the United Arab Republic or of interfering with Western oil interests, the United States hastened to accord it full diplomatic recognition.

As the result of Anglo-American policy, the West has, for the time being at least, lost practically all influence over the social and economic revolution now sweeping the Middle East. It is true that the oil-producing states need the Western market as much if not more than the West needs Middle East oil. But the highly profitable terms upon which the Western companies have been obtaining Middle East oil are in jeopardy. The monopoly itself is unlikely to continue long, unless means are found to spread the benefits of oil production throughout the area and unless the producing companies take steps to permit consumer access at reasonable prices to the enormous reserves under their control.

The point to be made here is that, partly because of its identification of the national interest of the United States with the interest of the oil monopoly, and partly because of its failure to understand the revolution taking place in the Middle East, the American government has not only failed to divert Britain from an unwise and obsolete policy but has adopted that policy as its own. Britain at least had the excuse that she was dependent for her life upon Middle East petroleum. The United States, with its vast domestic and Latin-American oil resources, had no such excuse. In addition, Britain was, during the postwar period, mastering the difficult psychological as well as economic problems of dismantling a colonial empire. The United States faced no such problem; its failure to understand and win the allegiance of the awakening peoples of the Middle East was due to its obsessive preoccupation with the military containment of communism and its predilection for maintaining the global *status quo*.

Thus, whereas one might say that, with respect to Asia, Britain failed the United States in not persuading it to a wiser course, the reverse has been true with respect to the Middle East.

In Europe, on the other hand, there has been close Anglo-American policy co-ordination. This was the natural outcome of World War II and of subsequent American aid to European recovery. For better or worse, depending upon one's point of view, Britain and the United States originally saw eye to eye as to the postwar treatment of Germany, but in recent years both Britain and Canada have supported Washington's inflexible policy with increasing reluctance. The Labour Party in Britain and the Liberal Party in Canada—both at present in opposition—have strongly urged a greater willingness to negotiate with Moscow and to consider some form of disengagement in Central Europe. Even the Conservative governments in both countries have evidenced some loss of confidence in the American thesis of negotiating only from a "position of strength."

Unfortunately this moderating British-Canadian influence has been more than offset by the attitude of the West German Adenauer government, which has been even less willing than Washington to consider German neutralization. Nevertheless, even in West Germany there are signs that no one other than the venerable and determined Chancellor could long hold the Federal Republic to the rigidly uncompromising course prescribed by Washington.

Anglo-American policy toward France during the period of the Fourth Republic has done little toward helping the French to solve their problems. Washington and London pushed a reluctant France into an agreement permitting West Germany to rearm as a partner of NATO, thereby adding to French fears and to the cleavages in French public opinion. Instead of helping France to develop a more enlightened colonial policy, the United States encouraged the French to continue the war in Indochina to the bitter end and, even after that disastrous experience, did little or nothing to prevent its repetition in North Africa. Britain, for its part, remained aloof from the European Coal and Steel Community and from the efforts of France, West Germany, Italy, and the Benelux countries to establish a common market.

The demise of the Fourth Republic and the accession to power of Charles de Gaulle have marked a decisive turning point both in French internal affairs and in French colonial policy, giving hope of a stronger and more stable France and perhaps the development of something like a French Commonwealth. But these hopes hang precariously upon the skill, determination, and endurance of one man.

More than ever, the uncertainties of the European future demand alert and united Anglo-American action.

The major political problems facing the Anglo-American alliance may, then, be summarized in these abbreviated terms:

In the Far East, there is urgent need for an Anglo-American policy directed at coming to terms with the Chinese revolution; at making it possible for Japan to earn her living through liberal trade; and at aiding Southeast Asia—especially India—to prove that it is not necessary for Asian peoples to adopt communism in order to achieve satisfactory social and economic progress.

In the Middle East and North Africa, Britain and the United States must recognize that it is impossible to fight both communism and Arab nationalism; that the West must come to terms with Arab nationalism and seek to reach an agreement with the Soviet Union to leave the future of the Arab world in the hands of the Arab peoples, with all economic assistance stripped of political overtones. Having sponsored the creation of a Jewish state in the Middle East, the United States and Britain must recognize their obligation to assist its peaceful integration in the area, ceasing to regard Israel as in any sense a bridgehead of the West. Throughout the area, the Anglo-American aim must be to establish peace rather than influence, and to aid rather than to obstruct inevitable change.

With respect to Europe, it is necessary for the United States and Britain to reappraise a policy which has rested far too heavily upon obsolete strategic concepts and which has run into a dead-end street. The key to the future of Europe lies in a German settlement and in the ultimate relationship between Germany and France. The nature of this relationship will depend upon whether Germany is reunited and militarily neutralized, or whether a militarized, economically resurgent and irredentist West Germany dominates the Western part of a divided Europe and again looms as a potential threat to peace. In addition, Anglo-American policy requires readjustment to the dramatic changes taking place within France and in French relations to Africa.

The future of the African continent is closely linked to that of Europe and the Middle East. Whether the rapidly awakening peoples of Africa ally themselves with the West or turn against it hinges chiefly upon three factors: upon the rapid, peaceful achievement of Algerian independence; upon generous and effective Western aid to the development of the emerging African nations; and upon the success or failure of the West in eliminating from the African areas of white settlement the cancer of *apartheid* and racial discrimination. Without firm Anglo-American backing for a liberal French colonial policy—without generous Anglo-American support of the newly independent African nations—and without decisive Anglo-American pressure against racialism, it is unlikely that these three conditions will be fulfilled.

The emphasis thrown in this chapter upon the need for more effective Anglo-American co-operation is not intended to suggest a weakening of Anglo-American ties to or co-operation with other nations. On the contrary, it is aimed at making such co-operation more effective.

The conviction underlying this emphasis is that, in a rapidly changing world, the English-speaking peoples—together with some of the more stable smaller nations—are least likely to be distracted by internal upheavals and, therefore, most likely to be able to contribute toward guiding inevitable change in the direction of peace.

CHAPTER TEN

The Anatomy of Failure

What lies at the root of the failure of the United States either fully to understand the nature of the mid-twentieth-century crisis or to take advantage of the opportunities which it presents for constructive leadership?

Europeans are inclined to blame American ignorance of history and of present-day world conditions, American emotionalism, and an American predilection for thinking that there must be a quick solution for every problem that arises.

Asians and Africans are inclined to place the emphasis upon American failure to understand that the American system is not applicable to other less fortunate peoples, upon an American sense of racial superiority, and upon American *status quoism*.

The peoples of the Arab Middle East see the United States as the successor to European imperialism and as the chief sponsor and supporter of Israel as an imperialist bridgehead in the Arab world.

We must ask ourselves what factors within the United States give rise to these impressions?

Much has been said and written about the influence of special-interest pressure groups upon the shaping of American foreign policy. It is true that at times some of these groups exercise a disproportionate and not always constructive influence. For example, consideration for "the Catholic vote" inhibited President Roosevelt from giving aid to the Spanish Republic; the Zionist lobby caused President Truman to act more impulsively than he otherwise might have with regard to the partition of Palestine; the China lobby has exerted great pressure for the maintenance of the alliance with Chiang Kai-shek; the textile lobby has fought against according Japan a fair share of the American market; and the perennial protectionist lobby has impeded all tariff revision. On the other hand, pressure-group activities have supported the Marshall Plan, the Point Four program, and adherence to the United Nations. On the whole, citizen pressure groups tend to balance each other out and, in any case, they provide almost the only way by which individual citizens in a mass democracy can exercise any influence whatever upon the formation of national policy. In some ways, pressure-group activity by citizens ganging up together to promote a common interest or a common cause provide a better expression of the popular will than the formal machinery of representative government.

There are, however, certain quite specific and curable defects in the American policy-making process to which it may be useful to draw attention.

1. The American system provides no recognized focus of opposition leadership and no suitable machinery for effective formulation of opposition policy.

In theory, the defeated candidate for President is the titular head of the opposition until the nomination, four years later, of its candidate for the next election. In practice, opposition leadership is fragmented, especially when a former President belonging to the party out of power is still living and active in politics. Since 1953, Mr. Truman has exercised at least as much influence as Governor Stevenson, the titular head of the Democratic Party.

Actually, opposition policy with respect to foreign affairs has, in recent years, been shaped almost entirely by the congressional leadership. This has been true irrespective of which party has been in power. From 1933 to 1953, when the Democrats were in power, the Republican attitude toward foreign policy was shaped chiefly by such powerful Senators as Robert

A. Taft and Arthur E. Vandenberg and by the Republican leadership in the House, rather than by former President Hoover, Governor Landon, Wendell Willkie, or Governor Dewey, successively the titular heads of the party.

The preponderance of congressional influence upon the opposition's foreign-policy position has been due, in part, to the fact that appropriations have come to play such a large part in the shaping of foreign policy, thus giving Congress a far greater voice in the conduct of foreign relations than was originally intended or than Congress possessed when foreign affairs made little demand upon the public purse. But that is not the whole story.

The main reason why opposition policy is dominated by congressional leadership is that the American system provides no "opposite number" to the President who can effectively lead in the formulation of opposition policy. Not only is the titular head of the party out of power not ordinarily a member of Congress, but, under the American system, he is provided with no financial support or facilities of any sort. Unless he happens to be a man of independent means, the titular head of the opposition must devote much or most of his time to earning a living. He must pay out of his own pocket for whatever staff or secretariat he maintains. His means of keeping in touch with what is happening in the world are not much better than those of the ordinary citizen.

This is a major defect which could easily be remedied, especially as former Presidents are now to be paid a salary for life. A former President has no specific responsibility, though his experience qualifies him to give advice if he feels so inclined; he is certainly entitled to a reward for past services. But the titular head of the opposition party has, or should have, a responsibility which, in the existing circumstances, he finds it almost impossible to fulfill.

2. Since 1953 a distorted form of so-called bipartisanship in foreign policy has resulted in the absence of constructive criticism on the part of the Democratic leadership in the Congress.

There are times of national emergency when it is desirable to have the nation united behind a coalition policy, but a true coalition policy is one which is hammered out by compromise between the party in power and the party in opposition. This is what the United States had during World War II and afterward, when Senator Arthur Vandenberg of Michigan headed the Republican opposition during the administration of President Truman. There has been no such thing since the Republicans have been in power and the Democrats have been the opposition party. A handful of individual Democratic Senators—such as Fulbright of Arkansas, Humphrey of Minnesota, Kennedy of Massachusetts, Monroney of Oklahoma, Morse of Oregon, and Sparkman of Alabama—have put forward and worked hard for important elements of an alternative foreign policy. Similar good work has been done by a group of younger Democrats in the House, led by Congressman Henry Reuss of Wisconsin. But these men are mavericks in their party. Under the leadership of Lyndon Johnson in the Senate and Sam Rayburn in the House—both from Texas—the bulk of the Democratic opposition in the Congress has, broadly speaking, taken a position on foreign policy which amounts to saying: "We'd do the same thing, only we'd do it harder and better." The emphasis has been upon criticism of execution, not upon the basic conception of foreign policy.

Clearly, this attitude on the part of the majority of the Democrats in Congress has derived in part from a reluctance to disagree with policies originated by the Truman administration. The same consideration understandably hampered Governor Stevenson in 1952 and again—less understandably—in 1956. Yet one need not share this observer's view that substantial parts of the Truman policy were ill conceived from the start, in order to recognize that, no matter how wise these policies may have been when initiated, they have long been obsolete and irrelevant.

3. The Democratic Advisory Committee was formed in 1957 presumably as a counterfoil to the politically astute but unimaginative and uncreative Johnson-Rayburn leadership. But this distinguished group of Democratic leaders has produced very little in the way of a domestic program and, so far as

foreign policy is concerned, has allowed former Secretary of State Dean Acheson to become its spokesman.

Unfortunately Mr. Acheson's originally fertile and creative mind seemed to have become imprisoned in the past. He apparently felt that any drastic revision of foreign policy, except as to China, would reflect upon the Truman administration. There was no evidence to suggest that Mr. Acheson realized either that some of his own policies, such as his policy with respect to Germany, might have been ill conceived or—assuming their wisdom at the time—that they might now be out of date. Mr. Acheson effectively and often caustically criticized policy execution, but until the second crisis over the Chinese offshore islands, in September 1958, there appeared to be less substantive difference between the former Secretary of State and his successor than between Mr. Acheson and the Democratic mavericks in the Congress.

When Mr. Acheson did take a firm and effective stand against American involvement over Matsu and Quemoy, his former chief, Mr. Truman, openly disagreed with him, while the titular head of the party, who had spoken out forcefully against such involvement in 1955, remained silent during the critical period.

On the whole, Democratic leadership has shown neither originality nor initiative since the party has been in opposition. This, plus a lack of respect for the creative mavericks within the party, has made the opposition accessory to most of the errors committed by the party in power.

With Senator Fulbright's accession to the chairmanship of the powerful Senate Foreign Relation's Committee, there is reason to hope that we shall see a change for the better.

In addition to the absence of a properly functioning "loyal opposition," there has been a notable absence of a nationwide opposition press, such as exists in most European democracies. Whether this has been a contributing cause of distorted bipartisanship or its result, it is difficult to say. The fact itself, however, is noteworthy.

It is also highly significant that during the second Eisenhower administration a Democrat-controlled Congress has to an unprecedented extent handed over to the Executive the power to make or risk war. Secretary Dulles has been permitted to commit the United States all over the globe, often merely by Executive agreements not subject to Senate ratification. The President, acting under the resolution approving the so-called Eisenhower Doctrine, was enabled to land troops in Lebanon at his sole discretion; and the decision whether or not to go to war with China over Matsu and Quemoy was explicitly handed over to the President in January 1955 by a vote of 410 to 3 in the House and 85 to 3 in the Senate. Never before in the history of the United States has there been such an abdication of constitutional power on the part of Congress.

4. The sterility of the opposition and the absence of criticism in the press at an extremely critical time like 1958 would have been less important if the party in power had been capable of strong, imaginative leadership. One has to turn back the pages of American history by a full century, to the days when James Buchanan occupied the White House, in order to discover a time when the United States faced a desperate crisis under leadership as weak, complacent, and unimaginative as that from which it has suffered under the Eisenhower administration. Nor has there probably ever been a time in American history when the people, irrespective of weak or strong leadership, have been as passive in the face of mounting danger as they were until the late summer of 1958.

The passivity of the American people—a strange compound of acute anxiety and an almost somnambulistic euphoria—was no doubt the product of such factors of frustration as were discussed in Chapter Two in connection with the crisis of democracy. But there is also a circular connection between weak leadership and public apathy—between a do-nothing administration and a popular desire to push the unpleasant facts of life under the rug, even when the rug is worn so threadbare as to be almost nonexistent. Each phenomenon feeds upon the other. When the people are in a state of euphoria, they tend to elect to office amiable men most likely to offer them the reassuring platitudes they desire to hear, rather than serious men who might disturb their tranquillity. And when amiable men are thus elected to leadership, they tend to nourish the euphoric state upon which their popularity depends.

The result, in time of crisis, is disastrous.

In the particular crisis of our time, the result has been the freezing into sterile immobility of American foreign policy during a period of world-wide revolutionary change, and the wholly unnecessary and preventable slipping of the American economy into a serious even though temporary slump, at a time when failure to prevent an economic setback in the United States was equivalent to letting a fire break out in the central firehouse of the Western community.

When the crisis came, in 1958, American foreign policy reflected not only weak leadership, the absence of a properly functioning opposition and public apathy, but a sagging economy, a lagging social development, and, above all, the fact that the intellectual vitality of the nation has been stifled in widespread conformity to a know-nothing, do-nothing state of wholly unwarranted complacency.

5. Perhaps the most serious obstacle standing in the way of correcting these conditions was the fact that the American people were not being told the truth.

Since 1953 it has been impossible for any reasonably well-informed independent observer to recognize the world as described from time to time by the highest officials of the American government. In President Eisenhower's rare utterances and especially in the more frequent reports of the Secretary of State to the Congress or to the people, diplomatic encounters which had appeared to the outside observer as re-sounding defeats have somehow turned into splendid victories; developments which seemed to furnish ominous evidence of communist strength have been transmuted into proof of communist weakness; and apparent indications of the crumbling of one or more of Mr. Dulles' many alliances have been metamorphosed into manifestations of strength and unity.

In May 1958 the Senate Foreign Relations Committee began a long-overdue investigation designed to lay the foundations for a serious re-examination of United States foreign policy.

Four Assistant Secretaries of State appeared as witnesses to set the stage for the appearance of Mr. Dulles. Each defended American policy in his particular bailiwick. One went so far as to assert that in his area, Europe, "the success of American policy" had been "nothing short of miraculous."

On the following day, June 4, 1958, the writer appeared as a witness summoned by Chairman Theodore Green of Rhode Island to testify as an outside observer. The following is a brief excerpt from his testimony:

> When Secretary Dulles testifies at the conclusion of these hearings, I have no doubt that he will say once more, as he has frequently said in the past, that he sees no reason to reconsider any of his basic premises and policies. If so, he will in truth outdo the Roman Emperor Nero, who is said to have fiddled while Rome burned but who, so far as I know, never appeared before the Roman Senate to deny that the city was on fire.
>
> The blunt truth, which I do not think you will hear from Mr. Dulles, is that, if the West does not quickly put its own house in order, it will be too late to negotiate with Russia about disengagement, disarmament or anything else. The West will have nothing left with which to negotiate.
>
> It is not just this or that piece of our foreign policy that needs overhauling. The whole of it is bankrupt; and its bankruptcy endangers not merely the security of the United States but the survival of civilized life upon this planet.

No dissent from this blunt appraisal was voiced by any of the Senators present.

Two days later, on June 6, Secretary Dulles appeared as the final witness. Unruffled by recent events, the Secretary of State presented the committee with an ideal banker's balance sheet showing all assets and no liabilities. The assets consisted of the alleged successes of American foreign policy plus a catalogue of the supposed weaknesses of the communist dictatorships. There was no mention of any failure on the part of American diplomacy and no recognition of any mistakes. Naturally there was no reason, according to Mr. Dulles, to re-examine policies which had achieved such remarkable success.

This was at a time when Vice-President and Mrs. Nixon had just returned from their unhappy experience in Latin America, when the French-Algerian crisis was moving to its climax, and when the revolt against the pro-Western government of Lebanon had been on the front pages for some time.

Assuring the committee that he could see no reason whatever for a basic revision of American foreign policy in any part of the world, the Secretary of State proclaimed:

"We are not being tossed about rudderless on a sea of change. We are guiding and influencing change so that it shall be constructive."

Just where had the United States been guiding change into constructive channels? In Asia, where Indonesia, Burma, Laos, and Cambodia were drifting toward communism? In Latin America, where the Vice-President of the United States had just been stoned and spat upon? In France, slipping into a dictatorship of the Right? In Algeria, seething with revolt? In Greece, where the communists had just gained seventy-two seats against none in previous elections? Or in the Middle East, where the situation was deteriorating so rapidly that within six weeks United States marines would land in Lebanon?

Surely it was amply evident that, far from guiding change into constructive channels, the United States had, in fact, been futilely resisting change and vainly attempting to prop up the rickety remnants of the past.

How can the American people form sound judgments—how can the Congress act intelligently—when the highest foreign-policy-making officials either cannot see the truth or else willfully conceal it?

The members of Congress are harassed by a deluge of mail, overwhelmed by the demands of their constituents, and burdened with so many committee assignments that it is almost impossible for even the best of them to do any constructive, consecutive thinking about world affairs. Their personal and committee staffs are inadequate to do independent research. Congress has no choice but to rely upon the well-staffed Executive Branch for the factual information upon which to base its foreign-policy judgments.

The failure of Congress adequately to support wise policies and constructively to oppose unwise Executive proposals in the field of world affairs is very largely due to the fact that in recent years Congress has not only been inadequately informed but actually misinformed and misled by the Executive.

It is true that any Congressman or private citizen can, if he has the time, gain a fairly good picture of the facts by carefully reading the newspapers and listening to one of the better radio stations. But with a few notable exceptions among the news analysts and commentators (such as Walter Lippmann, Eric Sevareid, Edward R. Murrow and a few others), the mass media have not been very effective in counteracting the self-righteous complacency which has colored the information emanating from the White House and the Department of State. The mass media present the facts, but they rarely point out where the facts are at variance with official statements.

6. The lack of a critical evaluation of Executive reports concerning world affairs is especially evident at precisely those moments when it is particularly important that the facts be clearly understood. At such moments there is apt to be a curious conspiracy of silence, arising partly out of a perverted sense of patriotism and partly out of the legacy of fear left behind by the era of McCarthyism, in which dissent was muted lest it be equated with disloyalty.

Nineteen Fifty-eight furnished two examples.

When the Executive Branch and its intelligence services were caught completely by surprise over the revolution in Iraq and when Congress was faced with the accomplished fact of the landing of American marines in Lebanon, a single Congressman—Henry Reuss of Wisconsin—arose in the House of Representatives to state that in his opinion this precipitate action was both unwise and dangerous, only to be told by Speaker Rayburn that such comments were inappropriate at such a time. In the Senate the usual handful of maverick Democrats and two courageous Republicans—Flanders of Vermont and Cooper of Kentucky—expressed their misgivings. Republican minority leader, Knowland of California, hailed the President's action. Democratic majority leader, Lyndon Johnson of Texas, defended the landing and said: "Whatever the future may hold in store for us, the American people will be united behind the President." The assistant majority leader, Mansfield of Montana, questioned the "wisdom of landing American marines in Lebanon at this time" but promised his "very best support." Former President Truman supported the administration's action. Governor Stevenson was out of the country.

Although the landing was only the first step in a risky adventure, those who deeply doubted its wisdom felt constrained to temper their remarks as if the nation were already at war, and as if all responsibility for any future action had already been taken out of their hands.

Contrast this behavior with that of the Labour opposition in the House of Commons a day later, when Prime Minister Macmillan presented Parliament with the accomplished fact of a British landing in Jordan. A full-dress debate ensued, with the Labour leadership expressing sharp criticism and insisting upon a vote which, if carried, would have repudiated the government's action. Mr. Hugh Gaitskell, the opposition leader, demanded that the government at least make an attempt to reach a mutual hands-off agreement with the Soviet Union before taking action which might lead to a major conflict. When it came to the vote, all but six members of the opposition, who abstained, voted against the government. Prime Minister Macmillan was sustained by a margin of only sixty, with the Conservatives voting for him on strict party lines.

It does not matter whether or not one agrees with the substantive position taken by the British opposition leaders. The point is that they took a position, and not out of partisanship but out of deep concern over what they considered a dangerous mistake. Unable to stop the first move in what seemed to them a wrong policy, they undertook at once to mobilize public support for their demand that an attempt be made to come to terms with the Soviet Union. They did not, like the opposition leaders in the United States, act as if their country were already at war.

The direct consequence of the opposition's action was to force

Prime Minister Macmillan to override the wishes of the United States in agreeing to a "summit meeting" at the United Nations. Whether this was, in itself, wise or foolish is beside the point. The point is that, as against a supine opposition in the United States, the opposition in Britain took the initiative and proposed an alternative course which evoked a response from an informed public opinion and strongly influenced government policy.

The second example of distorted patriotism was furnished by the attitude of the administration during the Quemoy crisis of August–October 1958.

In contrast to the Middle East crisis, in which the Congress and the people were confronted with the accomplished fact of the landing in Lebanon, the Quemoy crisis presented an opportunity for discussion before any irrevocable steps had been taken. As stated in Chapter Eight, public opposition was mobilized with considerable effect, in spite of the lamentable performance of opposition leadership.

The nationwide outpouring of dissent from the policy being pursued by the Eisenhower administration evoked an official response which could only be described as petulant and wholly lacking in respect for dissenting opinion. President Eisenhower, in a nationwide telecast, spoke of "misguided people" who disagreed with his policy, accusing them of being "appeasers" and comparing them to those who, in 1938, had advocated the betrayal of Czechoslovakia. Vice-President Nixon not only denounced as a saboteur the State Department official who released the facts as to public protest but said, in effect, that public opinion should not be accepted as a guide to foreign policy. And when the venerable chairman of the Senate Foreign Relations Committee—since retired—privately wrote the President expressing his misgivings, the President replied in an angry letter released to the press that the Senator was in effect encouraging the Chinese Communists to believe that the American people would not stand behind their government in the event of war.

All this was unpleasantly reminiscent of the unhappy era of McCarthyism, when dissent from any part of official anti-communist policy was at once equated with treason. It was a healthy sign of recovery from this dismal period of American history that the administration's attitude, far from squelching dissent, served only to make dissent more widespread and more articulate—so articulate, in fact, that the administration was compelled to retreat from its extreme position. This may be a hopeful omen for the future.

The fact remains, however, that public opinion in the United States labors under considerable difficulty. Even when the British government has acted foolishly—as it did, in this observer's opinion, when it undertook the invasion of Egypt—it has acted for reasons which the British public could understand and which public opinion was, therefore, in a position to accept or reject. This has not, in recent years, been the case in the United States. Even when the American government has acted wisely, the American people have been befuddled by broad generalities, moralistic constructions, and complicated legalisms. Whatever the United States undertakes—be it wise or foolish—is rationalized not in terms of a clearly defined policy based upon stated facts but in terms of a crusade. (And, incidentally, what less appropriate word could be employed to describe a policy aimed at peace?)

7. Throughout the postwar period, national policy has not been explained to the Congress and the people. It has been "sold" by an appeal to fear and hatred rather than by an appeal to reason.

This is the psychology of war, not the psychology of peace.

There has been nothing more revolting on the American scene in recent years—unless it be the spectacle of Little Rock—than the manner in which the best instincts of the American people have been distorted and betrayed by the promotion of this war psychology.

What could be more shameful than the annual, ritualistic battle between those members of the Congress who rally to the support of wholly inadequate administration proposals for economic aid to the underprivileged two thirds of humanity and those members of Congress who oppose these proposals and seek to cut them down? For months each year this debate rages, with one side shouting: "Stop the giveaways!" and the other shouting back: "If we don't continue foreign aid, we shall lose the cold war to the communists!"

And what is this Donnybrook about? It is about a niggardly administration proposal amounting to less than one tenth of 1 per cent of the nation's annual income!

While two thirds of the world's population live on the ragged edge of starvation, this truly disgusting annual exhibition takes place in a country in which fortunes are made out of weight-reducing pills, slimming diets, and slenderizing establishments.

Each year the administration blames the Congress for cutting down its puny proposals, and each year Congress takes refuge in the allegation that there is no public support for foreign aid. How can there be? How can there be public interest in a debate over whether a few more pennies should or should not be pinched from a paltry, fear-inspired program which aims at little more than a defensive purpose?

It would not be difficult to win public support for a generous, imaginative, humanitarian program. There is in the American people a vast, untapped reservoir of compassion and humanitarian good will. If public support for foreign economic aid has been lacking, it is because the puny programs presented have been supported by all the wrong arguments—by arguments which focus the public's attention not upon the relief of suffering masses of humanity but upon the satanic image of the cold-war enemy.

The policy of secrecy, of non-disclosure, and of dishing out unwarranted reassurances, instead of factual information, destroys the very foundation of democracy, which is an alert and informed citizenry. It creates waves of apathetic complacency alternating with waves of hysterical fear, instead of a public opinion based upon comprehension and reason.

Writing about the United States a century and a quarter ago, Alexis de Tocqueville warned against the coming of that time when "each individual man becomes more like all the rest, more weak and more insignificant," and when government acquires a habit of "ceasing to notice the citizens to consider only the people, and of overlooking individuals to think only of their kind."

Western civilization is based upon Individual Man.

When Western governments cease to respect Individual Man, thinking of "the people" as an amorphous, faceless mass to be collectively manipulated rather than individually informed, then Western civilization is in danger. Once the pluralism of mass democracy is forgotten, the citizenry becomes a mob, and democracy ceases to exist.

There are enough factors which unavoidably tend to depreciate Individual Man in a mechanized, corporation-dominated modern society, without adding the fatal downward pressure of denying Individual Man the right to know the facts concerning the complicated world in which he lives.

If the ultimate challenge to Western civilization is to cause humanism and reason to become the operative elements in place of fear and hate, then it must be remembered that a mob can easily be taught to hate and fear but that only Individual Man is capable of reason, love, and compassion.

CHAPTER ELEVEN

The Foundation for Success

I

The provision of full and accurate information concerning the swiftly changing world is only one part of that process of education which aims—or should aim—at making Individual Man into a rounded, humane, creative, and responsible member of society. This process begins in the home, continues through formal education, and should, ideally speaking, continue throughout adult life. Whether it does so continue depends to a large extent upon how the individual members of a society use their leisure time.

Since the launching of the Soviet sputniks in the autumn of 1957, much has been said and written about the need to revise and strengthen the American educational system. Americans and other Westerners discovered with something of a shock—though the facts had long been available—that the Soviet Union was producing more scientists and engineers each year than the supposedly unchallengeable United States. The general reaction was that "something has got to be done."

It was perfectly true—and had been long before the sputniks appeared in the heavens—that something needed to be done about the American school system. In the world's wealthiest country, there was in 1958 an estimated shortage of 220,000 teachers and 130,000 classrooms. Forty-six thousand teachers were being paid less than $2,500 per annum. More than

2,300,000 American children were attending school in over-crowded classrooms or makeshift facilities such as basements or converted garages. Many more attended only half-day school sessions because of the shortage of classrooms and teachers. With 45–50 children in a class, as was the case in many schools, how could a teacher be expected to teach or a child to learn?

There was no doubt that something needed to be done. There was also no doubt that nothing much would be done so long as the American people continued to regard lower taxes as more important than higher standards of education.

The dearth of teachers was not solely due to their being disgracefully underpaid. It was due at least as much to the fact that, in an era of anti-intellectual conformism, the social status of the teacher had sunk to an all-time low and that the joy had been taken out of teaching by know-nothing school boards which insisted upon the avoidance of what they called "controversial subjects."

What is there to teach if controversial matters are taboo? What is there in history, in philosophy, in religion, and, for that matter, in science that is not controversial? What is there for a young mind to learn except how to get lost in the woods of controversy and then to find the way out to an individual conclusion?

The sputnik-inspired demand for "greater emphasis upon science" is likely to make matters worse rather than better. A scientist without an inner-directed philosophy, moral sensibility, and humane sympathy is a dangerous member of society. Science itself, without philosophy to direct the use of scientific discovery, is a menace. The truly great scientists have, first of all, been great humanists, for whom discovery has meant the relief of suffering, the freeing of men from ignorance and superstition, and the opening up of new domains for creative human endeavor.

The function of basic education in a free society is not to teach skills of one sort or another but to produce the kind of men and women who will use whatever skills they may acquire for humane purposes.

The United States does not lack scientists and technicians.

It lacks a framework of purpose and morality within which to direct scientific and technological progress.

Whether or not this is true of other Western countries and of the West as a whole, the writer is not competent to judge. There can be no doubt, however, that the aims and methods of Western education are in need of careful re-examination; that in some countries the school system needs to be dragged out of hidebound tradition, while in others it needs to be reawakened to old values which have been neglected and forgotten.

One aspect of much-needed educational reform applies specifically to the United States and profoundly affects the relations of the United States to other countries.

The American educational system is woefully deficient in the teaching of languages and in providing the American child with even a rudimentary understanding of cultures, environments, and "ways of life" other than his own. In this respect the American educational system as a whole is still shaped to the needs of the self-contained American society as it was in the first decade of the twentieth century. It is wholly inadequate as a preparation for living in the modern, interdependent world.

The American lack of empathetic understanding, which so sadly hampers well-intentioned American efforts abroad, is the direct result of an educational system which teaches young Americans next to nothing about the relativity of their own values and experience to the value systems and experience of other peoples. The fact that Americans abroad so often feel themselves "misunderstood" is the corollary to their own inability to understand and accept anything that is "different."

In American secondary education there has in recent years been notable progress in what are called "language and area studies." Some American colleges now encourage students to take their junior year abroad. There has been some exchange of American and foreign students. But, as yet, these benefits affect only a small proportion of the American population.

At a time when the future of America is deeply involved in what may happen in Asia, in Latin America, in the Middle East, and in Africa, American education is still Europe-oriented in so far as it is oriented toward anything outside the United States.

The only languages taught are European languages, and even these are taught so poorly that the average American who goes to Europe, having "taken" French or Spanish or German, finds himself utterly unable to communicate, unless he can find someone who speaks English.

Obviously it is out of the question to teach every American child Russian, Chinese, Arabic, and Spanish, nor is this necessary. What is necessary is that every American child should acquire a real familiarity with at least *one* foreign language and culture. The important thing to learn is not factual knowledge but understanding—not every detail of the history and environmental factors affecting another people but the simple fact that different peoples have different histories, different environments, and different sets of values, and that deviation from the American norm does not imply inferiority.

Americans are going out into every corner of the world to teach technology, science, and religion. But effective teaching is half teaching and half learning. One cannot teach people whom one does not understand. What Americans lack is receptivity. They lack an education which equips them with respect for what is "different," with open-mindedness, with a predisposition to empathetic understanding, and, above all, with an ability to communicate.

This is true not only of the ordinary American citizen; it is also shockingly true of even those Americans who are especially "trained" for and sent out on foreign service. Only a tiny percentage of our ambassadors speak the language of the countries to which they are accredited. The same applies to most of the personnel of our diplomatic, economic, and military missions. As a consequence, American missions abroad depend heavily upon native personnel for translation of newspapers, radio broadcasts, and even confidential interviews or negotiations.

In most countries the natives who speak English represent the top social stratum of society—that is to say, a relatively privileged minority whose interest tends to lie in the direction of preserving the *status quo*. Thus the American diplomatic and economic missions often have no contact whatever with and no understanding of the revolutionary movements which are gaining strength under their very noses.

Instead of living in and learning to know a foreign country, Americans and their dependents stationed abroad tend to live with each other in isolated American ghettos, with their own schools, their PXs, their cocktail parties, and their own entertainment. Usually they have native servants and enjoy a living standard which bears no relation to that of the local people and which is often considerably higher than that which they would enjoy at home.

The result is that, even when they perform useful work, our foreign missions rarely earn the personal respect and liking of the peoples whom they are sent out to help.

Furthermore, the prevalence of native translators, assistants, and domestic servants often makes for an appalling lack of security. (Soviet missions are as a rule fully staffed by Soviet citizens, almost all of whom speak the language of the country to which they are sent.)

There are, of course, outstanding exceptions to these generalities, especially among the career men in the foreign service, but the exceptions are all too few.

The nationalistic parochialism of American education is largely responsible for the fact that the United States has become a *status quo* power in a rapidly changing world.

An educational system molded to the mental habits of a self-satisfied, self-contained, nineteenth-century American society has bred in the American people a predilection for what President Harding called "normalcy"—meaning a return to things as they were before an unwanted involvement in world affairs temporarily disturbed life in the United States. President Eisenhower has frequently expressed similar nostalgic longings. The self-centeredness of American education has produced in most Americans an almost infantile resentment of "outside" interference and a resistance to any development abroad which might conceivably affect the domestic scene.

Americans do not resent change if they themselves initiate it. Few peoples have, in fact, developed a more fluid society.

Americans, more than any other people, believe in "progress"—not only for themselves but for all the world's peoples. But they are as a rule utterly unable to recognize as "progress" any revolutionary change abroad which they think threatens to affect their "normal" pursuit of their own interests.

Ignorance of the world beyond their own borders has conditioned Americans to harbor a longing for a return to the time when whatever happened "outside" did not much matter. Yet Americans know that a return to those days is impossible; their unconscious longing for the *status quo ante* has been converted into a conscious determination at least to preserve the *status quo*. Isolationism has been converted into global interventionism directed toward maintaining things as they are.

One of the strange by-products of this *status quo* interventionism is American inability to see that what is sauce for the gander is sauce for the goose. American intervention in Lebanon or Guatemala is equated with a legal and laudable defense of national independence and the right of self-determination. Intervention by another power supporting revolutionary change is equated with aggression, either direct or indirect.

In other words, *status quoism* has created in the American mind the belief that the *status quo* is legal and that any change in the *status quo*—unless it be a change in the direction of restoring the *status quo ante*—is illegal.

Other factors besides an outmoded and essentially isolationist educational system have, of course, contributed to making the once revolutionary United States into a *status quo* power. Among these are the cold war and—perhaps even more important—the simple fact of American wealth and prosperity. Americans have, or think they have, more to lose through change than any other people. The same familiar motivation often makes wealthy individuals into ultra-conservatives.

The fact remains, however, that the American educational system is largely to blame for the fact that Americans still grow up in ignorance of the world around them; that this ignorance breeds the conviction that what is American is good, while anything that is "different" is probably less good; and that complacent provincialism engenders the suspicion, if not the outright fear, that any change in the world-as-it-is threatens American security.

There could be no greater mistake than to undertake the much-needed re-examination of the American school system solely from the point of view of competing more effectively with the Soviet Union in the arms race.

In a report written for Freedom House after a recent visit to the Soviet Union, Dr. Harry D. Gideonse, president of Brooklyn College, New York, made this pertinent observation:

> If we merely stress the financial and technical side of the Russian challenge, we might eventually end up by being as good as they are in the achievement of *their*, and *not of our*, purposes. This is a qualitative challenge and it is, first of all, a challenge to the values of American life . . . We can restore the cutting edge of our values only by emphasizing the moral and the value side of our cultural life.

In this writer's opinion, even more is needed than an effort to revitalize American values, ideals, and moral concepts. The effort must include an attempt to relate a revitalized American value system to the value systems of other cultures. The proper point of departure must be a deliberate search for methods and means by which American children may best be educated into fearless, humane, creative, and responsible citizens not merely of the United States but of the world.

Perhaps the single, most effective approach to the problem would be greatly to increase the exchange of students and teachers. What little has been done in this direction has already borne magnificent fruit. One need only see the changes wrought in an American boy or girl who has spent a year going to school abroad and living with a foreign family, to realize what might be accomplished on a large scale. The same thing is true of the all-too-few foreign students who have visited the United States.

Another approach to the same problem which has been tried on a small scale with great success, especially by the International Friendship League, is to encourage individual correspondence between young Americans and their contemporaries abroad. It has been shown that this method teaches world-mindedness not only to children but to their parents.

In some American communities an entire town or village has become interested in "adopting" a town or village in a foreign country.

The work of the American Friends Service Committee has been outstanding in stimulating any and all approaches to world citizenship.

The trouble is that much of what has been done so far has happened outside the American school system and reaches only a tiny proportion of American children, while most of the adult population has not enjoyed even these limited benefits.

II

The reorientation of the school system is inseparable from the revitalization of the home as the central core of education and from the reactivation of Western morality through the home or the church or through a combination of both.

The Western concepts of morality were originally founded upon religious conviction. Although the fundamentalist views of the origin of man and of the nature of man in relation to the universe have been shaken by scientific discovery, it is probably true that, for the majority of the Western peoples and certainly for the majority of Americans, the sense of what is right or wrong still derives from religious belief, no matter how attenuated.

So long as there remains an awareness of the existence of moral law, it does not, in the writer's opinion, greatly matter whether moral law is considered as a revelation of God's will or as the product of human experience over the centuries. What matters is that Western Man's moral sensibility be reawakened. What matters is that, in a society composed of individuals the majority of whom profess a religious belief, the church has failed lamentably to uphold moral law in terms relevant to the existing crisis of Western civilization.

The writer can speak only of the United States, where his work brings him into frequent contact with religious leaders.

With a few notable exceptions, he has found among Christian ministers and Jewish rabbis an extraordinary aloofness from the political events and trends which have been bringing the human race nearer and nearer to the abyss of destruction. Perhaps aloofness is not the right word, for these religious leaders do share the hopes, anxieties, and fears of their congregations. In that sense they are no more aloof than most citizens, but that is just the point: they conform to the general acceptance of things as they are, without as a rule having, as religious leaders, any special sense of moral responsibility.

By and large, the church in the American society stands in a consciously taken position of being above politics. "Render therefore unto Caesar the things that are Caesar's." Yet to be above or aloof from politics in the modern world is to disavow any interest in the survival of civilization. (The term "politics" is here used in the broader sense—not as referring to a partisan struggle for power in the town, city, state, or nation, but as denoting the conduct of a national government in dealing with other nations and peoples of the world.)

The fact with which the church in the United States has, in the writer's opinion, been insufficiently concerned is that the conduct of American foreign relations in the postwar period has created a climate of opinion in which the American people have been conditioned to accept moral atrocity as a normal and necessary part of their existence.

In a supposedly God-fearing society, who, if not the man of God, is to speak out against the packaging of moral atrocity in the wrappings of false patriotism and sanctimonious self-righteousness? Who, if not he, is to bear witness that it is a crime against humanity and against God for any nation to pollute the atmosphere, which all the world's peoples must breathe, in order to further its own experiments in mass murder and destruction.

Granted that all war is morally indefensible and that, until war is abolished, any nation, once it is threatened by aggression or involved in armed conflict, must make certain compromises between military necessity and moral principle. Granted further that it is the function of political leadership to make these compromises, seeking as best it can to distinguish between immoral action actually deemed essential to survival and immoral action undertaken merely for the sake of a more expedient pursuit of national objectives. Is it the function of religious leadership to join in making these compromises? Is it not rather the function of religious leadship to see that the immorality of certain acts, like that of dropping the first atomic bombs upon Japan, is clearly recognized—that it be understood that a moral crime is being committed, even though it be committed out of presumed necessity?

Is it not the function of the churches to exert every effort toward keeping patriotism within the bounds of morality? Are there not times when the priest, minister, or rabbi must breast the prevailing tide of opinion, distinguish between true and false patriotism, and, if necessary, declare: "My country, much though I love thee, thou art wrong"?

Admittedly, it takes courage to denounce actions or policies undertaken by the government and supported by majority opinion. There are many individual clergymen who have given evidence of such courage, but they are the exception rather than the rule.

These observations apply more to the impact of the individual American churches or synagogues upon their communities than to religious leadership at the regional or national level. Some of the leadership organizations have actively concerned themselves with national policy. The Quakers and Unitarians have been outstanding in this respect. Recently other religious leadership groups have begun to express constructive dissent from official policy. Methodist leadership has espoused the banning of nuclear tests and condemned American policy with respect to China. The Methodist Council of Bishops has said:

When our major concern is defense . . . we may survive for a time but we shall never win the war for the minds of men. The restless millions of the world await positive proposals . . . designed to establish lasting peace, continuing economic justice and abiding racial brotherhood . . . We play into Communist hands when we identify our humanitarianism with national self-interest.

Perhaps the most politically interesting pronouncement came from the national leadership of the Presbyterian Church, to which both President Eisenhower and his Secretary of State belong. In June 1958 the General Assembly at Pittsburgh had this to say:

A false and baneful doctrine is being persistently proclaimed; namely, that in the present world situation there are only two alternatives—either victory over the new Communist powers, or the annihilation of the traditional democracies. There was a time when Christians and Moslems fervently held that one group or the other had to be totally vanquished by force. But eventually they learned to live in the same world. At a later period, Protestants and Roman Catholics thought that one side or the other had to be wiped out. But the time came when they, too, learned to coexist as they do today . . . So, while striving for the freedom of all men, we today must coexist with Communist nations. In this nuclear age, the only alternative to coexistence is coextinction.

Then, in an obvious reference to the need for negotiation, the General Assembly of the United Presbyterian Church continued:

Wisdom teaches that in the pursuit of common understanding there can be no substitute for personal encounter. Estranged people must meet one another; they must talk to one another and strive to understand one another. They must probe the causes of their alienation. They must overcome enmity and distrust . . . When men who profess the Christian religion make no adequate provision for a face-to-face encounter with their enemies, they betray the religion which they profess.

Finally, calling for a reappraisal of the concept of freedom and the "contemporary myth of the free world," the Presbyterian Assembly declared:

By our actions we proclaim to the world that lands where human freedom is utterly dead can qualify for membership

175

in the "free world" simply by supplying military bases or strategic commodities. This kind of international hypocrisy should be abhorrent to Christians and in its presence the Church dare not keep silent.

These admonitions were worthy of consideration by the President and his Secretary of State.

The over-all failure of religion—in spite of the efforts of leadership groups—to keep moral sensibility alive in a period of moral atrophy is not due solely to uncritical acceptance of political compromises. One is entitled to suspect that it is due also to the fact that many of the churches, by standing aloof from and above politics in a period of intense, widespread anxiety, tend to give comfort rather than guidance. This is perhaps to be expected in a time when most people seek escape from the problems which confront them rather than help in finding their solution. Yet one may question whether the deep spiritual need of this perilous age is merely for peace of mind— and whether the church fulfills its mission by calming rather than stimulating the anxieties aroused by the world's headlong rush toward disaster. One may question whether spiritual leadership, any more than temporal leadership, performs a helpful service in nourishing a wholly unwarranted state of passive euphoria. Yet if the church stands above politics—if it refrains from applying moral judgment to national policy—it has little to offer except comfort, at a time when the crying need is for moral guidance.

Moral guidance need not by any means always consist of protest against wrongdoing. The abolition of racial discrimination or a policy of more generous aid to the underprivileged two thirds of humanity, such as has been discussed earlier in these pages, can be greatly encouraged by religious leadership, not on the basis of enlightened self-interest, but on the basis of the cardinal principles of religion itself. Who better than the religious leader can appeal to the fraternal instincts in human nature? Who better than he can bring moral support to the dictates of reason?

What has been said here of religious leadership is equally true of men and women in all walks of life who profess ethical convictions, whether or not religiously inspired. What the preacher can say to his congregation in church or synagogue, the parent can say to children in the home. Teaching morality is more effective than preaching it, and the teaching of moral sensibility to a child is perhaps more fruitful than anything else that a man or woman can do.

III

The writer has spoken to many audiences in many parts of the United States about most of the subjects discussed in this book, and especially about the responsibility of the individual in a free society.

Almost everywhere he has encountered one recurring objection: "I haven't time!"

A man says he is too busy with his business, a woman is too busy with her home, a minister is too busy with the affairs of his parish—"I haven't time to keep myself informed, much less to form any judgment about the complicated issues of national policy!"

One answer is that, if everyone is too busy to be a citizen, democracy ceases to exist.

Another answer is: "What will happen to your business, what will happen to your home and children, what will happen to the affairs of your parish, if the lights of civilization are extinguished?"

And a third answer is that most of us would find that we do have time—much more time than people have ever had before—if we but used it profitably instead of wasting so much of it in idleness or childish games or purposeless puttering.

Which is more important: to build your child a rumpus room or to build your child's character? To dress and do your fingernails with elaborate care or to study the day's developments? To lower your score at golf or to raise the level of your intelligence?

There are people, like the overworked country doctor, who really don't have time for anything but their work.

Can you claim to be one of them?

How much time do you spend watching television, and what programs do you see? Where do you open a newspaper after glancing at the front-page headlines? Sports? Stock market? Social news? Advertisements? How much time, if any, do you spend on the crossword puzzle? What type of front-page story, if any, do you go back and read carefully: the story of a sensational crime or the report of a famine in India?

Is it really time that you lack, or do you lack interest and a sense of personal involvement and individual responsibility?

These are blunt and perhaps irritating questions. But, unless citizens in Western democracies begin soon to ask themselves such questions, there is not much hope for the survival of the free society.

It is true that the modern age confronts the responsible citizen with difficult, complex, and mostly unfamiliar problems; that it places him at a distance from the democratic processes of policy formation; and that it demands that he do a vastly greater amount of homework in order to be able to meet his responsibility. But the modern age provides the responsible citizen with two essentials: it provides him with more information about the world he inhabits than has ever before been available, and it provides him with time in which to study.

The great question is: Will Western Man use his increased leisure to educate himself, or will he go on wasting it?

If the world escapes from the imminent threat of annihilation, the answer to this question may well determine whether Western civilization survives or perishes.

The ancient Greek word *skolé,* from which are derived the Latin, French, Spanish, German, and English words for "school," actually meant "leisure in which to learn." Plato stated explicitly that leisure to learn could be enjoyed only by those who had the means. In Plato's time all physical labor had to be performed by human beings or animals—much of it by pitiable wretches who worked as slaves in order that the privileged few might enjoy leisure.

Today, in the highly industrialized countries of the West, the necessity for prolonged physical labor by human beings has been all but eliminated. The privilege of learning at school has become the right of every child, and the opportunity to go on learning throughout adult life exists for the majority of the Western peoples. Leisure has vastly increased and is steadily increasing.

One might expect, therefore, that the education of Western Man should be making rapid progress, especially by comparison with those parts of the world where the individual's leisure is not much greater than that enjoyed by the majority of people in ancient times. Yet liberation from physical toil seems, during recent years, to have tended to increase idleness rather than to free Western Man to think, to learn, and to create.

There are, of course, notable exceptions, and the degree to which this broad generalization is true varies in the different countries of the West. Not all the peoples of the West entertain the same attitude toward the relationship between work and leisure. The French—in many ways the most mature among the Western peoples—tend to live by Aristotle's dictum: "We work in order to have leisure." The Germanic peoples are more inclined to the belief, expressed by Max Weber, that "one does not work to live; one lives to work," although in postwar West Germany the use of leisure has been to some extent Americanized—that is to say, converted into pursuits of pleasure not very different from those of the English-speaking peoples.

The Anglo-Saxon attitude toward leisure is essentially immature compared to that of either the French or to that which used to be prevalent in Germany.

The Englishman, depending upon his social and economic status, traditionally fox-hunts, shoots, fishes, and breeds racing animals, or plays games, sails, takes a punt on the river, and bets on horse and dog races. His leisure world is primarily masculine, whether he spends his time out of doors or sitting in his club or public house.

The American does many of the same things but is essentially a family man. His games often involve his wife and children.

Much of his time is spent driving the family car bumper to bumper with other family cars on the overcrowded highways. Instead of going to his club or pub, he spends hours sitting at home in front of his television set.

Thorstein Veblen, in his *Theory of the Leisure Class,* observed that "the temperament which inclines men to sports is essentially a boyish temperament." Since Veblen's day, the majority of Americans have become members of the "leisure class," if such it can now be called; and Veblen's observation nowadays applies not merely to the privileged few but to the nation as a whole. Veblen, were he contemplating the contemporary American scene, would doubtless admit that participation in games and sports is a healthy antidote to the increasingly sedentary life of the machine age. If men who no longer use their muscles in earning a living did not exercise them in recreational activity, the human body might atrophy altogether. But one can imagine Veblen saying that this justification hardly applies to spending one's leisure time sitting either in a grandstand or before a television set watching other men or animals exercise their muscles.

The fact is that, in spite of vastly increased leisure, the education of Western Man has lagged far behind his material progress. At a time when the life span is being prolonged and working hours and working life are being shortened, one might expect that people would read more, think more, and indulge in more frequent exchange of opinions and ideas. By and large, this does not seem to be the case. Few children nowadays grow up in the United States accustomed to hearing serious conversation among their elders. Literature, in recent years, has tended less to stimulate thought than to provide escape from reality— less to set a high standard of creativity than to elevate the vulgar, the sensational, and the commonplace. Only in the growing appreciation of good music does there seem to be a healthy countercurrent to the prevailing tide of intellectual laziness.

Instead of liberating Western Man for increased creative activity, the machine age appears to be enslaving him to bore-

dom from which he seeks escape either through purposeless
activity, or through passive acceptance of what is euphemisti-
cally described as entertainment.

IV

The essential problem faced by the peoples of the West in the
second half of the twentieth century is no different from that of
twenty-five hundred years ago, when the first great free society
flourished in Athens. Listen to what the Athenian Pericles said
to his fellow citizens:

> Unlike other cities, Athens expects every citizen to take
> an interest in public affairs; and, as a matter of fact, most
> Athenians have some understanding of public affairs. We
> do believe in knowledge as a guide to action; we have a
> power of thinking before we act, and of acting too, where-
> as many people can be full of energy if they do not think
> but, when they reflect, they begin to hesitate. We like to
> make friends abroad by doing good and giving help to
> our neighbors; and we do this not from some calculation of
> self-interest but in the confidence of freedom in a frank and
> fearless spirit. I would have you fix your eyes upon Athens
> day by day, contemplate her potentiality—not merely what
> she is but what she has the power to be, until you become
> her lovers. Reflect that her glory has been built up by men
> who knew their duty, and had the courage to do it. Make
> them your examples and learn from them that the secret
> of happiness is freedom, and the secret of freedom, cour-
> age.

Athens perished because her citizens, no longer taking an
interest in public affairs, grew careless, timid, and complacent
—because they lost the power of thinking before they acted,
and began to hesitate whenever they took thought. Athens
perished because she no longer made friends abroad by doing
good and giving help to her neighbors in the confidence of
freedom and in a frank and fearless spirit. Athens ceased to be
great when her citizens no longer contemplated her potenti-

ality but became smugly satisfied with what she was—when Athenians no longer remembered that the secret of happiness is freedom, and the secret of freedom, courage. . . .

And so this book ends where it began:

"The mortal threat to Western civilization is not the enemy without, but the enemy within."

THREE SUPPLEMENTARY NOTES TO CHAPTER EIGHT

I. A REBUTTAL OF CERTAIN ARGUMENTS AGAINST DISENGAGEMENT IN EUROPE

The following is an excerpt from the writer's testimony before the Senate Foreign Relations Committee on June 4, 1958:

Secretary Dulles asserts that we cannot rely upon Russian good faith in keeping any agreements we might make.

I submit that nations do not make agreements relying upon each other's good faith. They rely upon each other's intelligent pursuit of self-interest. History shows that the international agreements most likely to be broken are precisely those which are negotiated by one side or the other from a "position of strength"—that is, under some degree of duress. On the other hand, the agreements most likely to be kept are those negotiated on a give-and-take basis from a position of mutually recognized equality. The agreements which endure are those freely entered into because they serve the self-interest of both parties and thus become self-enforcing. That is the sort of agreement we should seek.

Secretary Dulles asserts, as the clincher for his argument against negotiation, that the Russians agreed to free all-German elections at the Geneva "summit conference" of 1955, and that they then repudiated their agreement.

As several responsible American and British reporters present at Geneva have pointed out, this is a distortion of fact. The chiefs of state agreed that Germany should be reunified by free elections "in conformity with the national interests of the German people and the interests of European security." They were unable to agree as to which of these two considerations should come first, the Russians maintaining that a European security agreement involving Germany's neutralization must precede all-German elections, while the West held that free all-German elections must be a condition precedent to any settlement. The ambiguous wording of the communiqué merely concealed the failure to reach agreement. . . .

Chancellor Adenauer, in arguing against disengagement, has produced his own red herring, alleging that a neutralized Germany would fall easy prey to communist subversion.

The Chancellor knows quite well that Germany is far more immune to communism than France or Italy. What he fears is not ideological but political seduction—that, once he is gone, German history may repeat itself; in other words, that a neutralized Germany may once more play off Russia against the West, or even play with Russia against the West. This danger exists. But the risk of such seduction will be infinitely greater so long as Germany remains partitioned, with the Kremlin able to hold out the bait of reunification. Thus, the only real political risk is actually magnified by further adherence to our present policy.

Chancellor Adenauer also contends that, if foreign troops are withdrawn prior to free all-German elections, the result will be to freeze the partition.

The reverse is nearer to the truth. A mutual withdrawal of foreign troops would create the only conditions in which German reunification could reasonably be expected to come about. The withdrawal of Soviet coercive power would almost certainly topple the East German communist regime. With an indigenous regime of whatever complexion in power, a drawing together of the two German states would be inevitable, leading toward economic and eventually political integration. Free all-German elections would then probably come about, not as a condition precedent, but as the culmination of a gradual process of reunification.

It is contended by some of the military experts that the neutralization of Germany would, in effect, destroy NATO.

This contention is denied by some of our own top military men and by such British authorities as Marshal of the Royal

Air Force Sir John Slessor and Captain Liddell-Hart. I shall make only this layman's comment:

In one way or another, the military arguments against disengagement all rest upon a concept of strategy which was obsolete when NATO was first organized. The basic contention is that Western Europe cannot be defended without German space and German manpower. This is true. But the implied corollary, that Western Europe *can* be defended against invasion *with* German help, is *not* true; nor has it been true at any time since our overhasty postwar demobilization.

The fact is, and has been all along, that the only way to defend Western Europe is to prevent its being attacked.

If the Russians ever had any intention of invading Western Europe—which I doubt—they have not been deterred by NATO's pitifully small ground and tactical air forces. They have been deterred by the certain knowledge that an attack upon Western Europe would unleash nuclear war with the United States. The same deterrent would apply to the invasion of any territory from which the Russians had withdrawn and which they had agreed to neutralize.

Finally, let me dispose of two arguments often brought up against disengagement by the last-ditch adherents of our present bankrupt policy.

The first reads: *"We mustn't neutralize Germany because that is just what the Russians want."*

The second runs: *"It's silly to suggest any such plan because the Russians will never agree to it."*

I submit that a proposition cannot be rejected upon the basis of two contradictory hypotheses. The blunt truth is that we don't know what the Russians want or would accept because we have never made an honest effort to find out. We have for nine years done nothing but repeat demands which we knew to be unacceptable.

II. THE BERLIN CRISIS

On December 8, 1958, the author submitted to Secretary Dulles, to Senate Majority Leader Lyndon Johnson and to the Senate Foreign Relations Committee a rough draft of a recommended reply to the Soviet note of November 27, 1958.

A letter of transmittal emphasized three points:

1. That the United States was now confronted with an extremely serious crisis at the most sensitive point of confrontation.

2. That the Soviet note outrageously distorted past history and put forward a clearly unacceptable proposal; but that it would be a dangerous mistake for the Western powers merely to refute the distortions, to reject the proposal and to reaffirm their now hopelessly obsolete position with respect to Germany.

3. That it was high time for the Western powers to take the initiative with a counterproposal which, if accepted, would eliminate Germany both as a possible future threat to peace and as a bone of contention; and that if such a proposal were put forward and were rejected by Moscow, it would incontrovertibly demonstrate to world opinion that the Soviet Union actually did not want any German settlement, no matter how fair.

Draft Reply to the Soviet Government

The Government of the United States has now carefully studied the Soviet Government's note of November 27th.

Beyond noting that, in its opinion, the Soviet note seriously distorts history, the Government of the United States does not wish to enter into fruitless controversy over what is past. Moreover, the Government of the United States recognizes that divergent interpretations of past events are in the circumstances to some extent inevitable.

In this Government's view, each of the four victorious powers which occupied Germany after Hitler's defeat has in some measure contributed to the failure of the four-power experiment and to the creation of the regrettable conditions which have since arisen. It will serve no useful purpose for either side to pretend that the other is solely responsible.

The state of affairs now existing as to Germany and as to Berlin is unsatisfactory to all concerned. It is unjust to the German people and a cause of dangerous tensions between the Western powers and the Soviet Union. It constitutes a threat to world peace. The United States is prepared to do its utmost, in a spirit of conciliation, to cooperate in whatever measures will permit the German people to reunite in peace and freedom under conditions which will eliminate Germany both as a threat to peace and as a bone of contention between the Soviet Union and the West.

This is no longer the relatively simple problem which it was thirteen years ago, when the victors had it in their power to impose a peace settlement upon a vanquished Germany. The Western powers have now acquired obligations and commitments to the Federal Republic of Germany and to the people of the Western Sectors of Berlin, while the Soviet Union has acquired obligations to the German Democratic Republic and to the people of East Berlin. Whatever settlement is now reached must, in order to be lasting, be acceptable not only to the Soviet Union and the Western powers but to the people of East and West Germany and the people of Berlin. Furthermore, there must be taken into consideration the interests of all Germany's neighbors and of Europe as a whole.

In the opinion of this Government, there can be no solution to the problem of a divided Berlin except in the context of a solution to the problems of a partitioned Germany and a divided Europe. This Government must, therefore, reject the Soviet Government's proposal of November 27th, concerning the future status of Berlin.

On the other hand, the United States is prepared to enter at once into serious negotiations which aim at an all-German settlement and a general European security agreement. The United States considers that the Polish Rapacki Plan, as revised on November 7th, would furnish a useful point of departure for such negotiations.

The revised Rapacki Plan, as this Government understands it, would provide for two stages in the creation of a militarily neutralized zone. In the first stage, there would be a standstill in the nuclear armament of West and East Germany, Poland and Czechoslovakia and of the Soviet and Western forces stationed in these four states. With this nuclear standstill in effect, negotiations would be entered into concerning the reduction of the conventional armaments of the four states and the step-by-step withdrawal from these four states of foreign armed forces. The second stage would provide for putting into effect the agreements reached as to conventional disarmament and withdrawal, as well as for the total elimination of nuclear weapons from a zone comprising Poland, Czechoslovakia and the two German republics. The Rapacki Plan envisages that both stages would be subject to suitable controls, by which this Government understands either United Nations or other neutral supervision.

The Governments of Great Britain, France and the United States would, if some such plan were agreed upon, be prepared to recommend to the Federal Republic of Germany that it withdraw from the NATO alliance, provided that Poland, Czechoslovakia and the German Democratic Republic would withdraw, with Soviet consent, from the Warsaw Pact. There would then have been achieved the military neutralization of the fours states comprised in the zone.

In this way, the path would be opened toward the eventual reunification of Germany and toward a peace treaty providing for its permanent military neutralization.

This Government recognizes that there can be no such German settlement so long as both sides continue to adhere to the frozen positions of the past, with the Western powers demanding free all-German elections as a condition precedent to reunification and the Soviet Union seeking to obtain within a reunified Germany a disproportionate position of power for the East German Communist apparatus. Accordingly, the Governments of France, Great Britain and the United States now express their willingness to let the two militarily neutralized German states proceed by their own methods and means toward reunification, provided that the Soviet Government will likewise agree not to interfere in any way in this process.

It is the view of this Government that the two German states have, during the past decade, developed along such different lines that reunification will be a slow process, probably leading through a gradual rapprochement to some sort of confederation before organic unification can be achieved. While free all-German elections would thus become the final act of reunification, rather than a condition precedent, it must be clearly understood and explicitly agreed by the Soviet Government that there shall be no foreign interference in such elections when and if they take place.

With respect to Berlin, the Governments of the United States, Great Britain and France, considering their moral and legal obligations to the inhabitants of the Western Sectors, must insist that the *status quo* be maintained at least until all foreign troops have been withdrawn from Poland, Czechoslovakia and the two German republics. At that time it may be possible to consider the Soviet Government's suggestion of making the Western Sectors into a free city under United Nations trusteeship, until such time as complete German reunification takes place and a peace treaty goes into effect.

The Soviet Government will note that the suggestions outlined above mark an important departure from the position taken in the past by the three Western Governments. It is to be hoped that the Soviet Government will reply to these suggestions in a like spirit of conciliation.

The Western replies, delivered at the end of the year, quite properly rejected the Soviet proposal, held that there could be no solution to the problem of Berlin except in the context of a solution to the problem of Germany, and made it clear that the Western powers, while ready to discuss the broader problem, would not do so under the threat of an ultimatum. On the other hand, while engaging in an elaborate refutation of the Soviet version of past history, the Western replies gave no indication

of willingness to depart from past inflexible positions in a give-
and-take negotiation.

On January 14, 1959, during Mr. Mikoyan's visit to Washington, the writer published an article in the *Washington Post
and Times Herald,* repeating the substance of the suggestions
put forward in the draft reply of December 8. In addition, this
article urged an agreement on the part of the Western powers
and the Soviet Union to refrain from any interference in an
eventual boundary settlement between the government of Poland and an all-German government, once the latter should
have come into existence.

A final settlement of the German-Polish frontier, freely ar-
rived at by direct negotiation, is essential to the establishment
of lasting peace in Europe. Based upon conversations with
both Poles and Germans, it is the writer's impression that—given
the absence of outside interference—only relatively minor re-
adjustments of the Oder-Neisse Line would be required to
reach a settlement sincerely accepted by both sides as just and
final.

III. QUEMOY AND MATSU

Text of the author's petition inserted as an advertisement in
the *New York Times* of September 25, 1958.

Call Congress at Once Mr. President!

Mr. President:
The United States now finds itself in a position in which it
can at any moment be committed to an utterly insane and
disastrous war by a single rash act on the part of either faction
in a Chinese civil conflict.

We consider this an intolerable situation.

Without arguing the merits or defects of our past bipartisan
policy with respect to the Nationalist-Communist struggle in
China, we point out two facts:

1. Our policy has been and is at variance with that of our
major anti-Communist allies and inconsistent with both govern-

ment and popular opinion in practically all of the crucially important uncommitted nations.

2. Our policy has remained static and inflexible throughout a decade in which profound changes have taken place and during which China—ten years ago a weak, strife-torn, and impoverished nation—has emerged into a highly organized, powerful state comprising one quarter of the world's population.

We profoundly regret that this change has come about under a ruthless Communist dictatorship, but our regret cannot alter the facts.

We emphasize that the radically modified circumstances have brought about no change whatever in a policy based upon the contention that the exiled Nationalist regime at Taipei is still the legitimate government of China and upon the hope of its restoration to power on the mainland.

We point out further that Chiang Kai-shek, to whom we are at present committed, rejects any and all settlements which would neutralize either the offshore islands or Taiwan itself; and that our commitment to support his position renders it impossible for us to come to any sort of peaceable settlement with the Chinese People's Republic.

It seems evident that a continuation of our present policy can lead only to a war in which the United States will have few if any effective allies, or to the indefinite protraction of a state of affairs in which the United States can at any moment be plunged into such a war by an act or decision other than its own. We are not persuaded that there is no alternative to this policy except "appeasement" or surrender.

We, therefore, feel justified in demanding that the whole of our China policy and all questions incident to our involvement in the Chinese civil conflict be laid before our elected representatives in the Congress, in whom the Constitution vests the power to decide upon war or peace.

We feel that the American people owe it to themselves and to humanity to decide upon their course by the democratic process, rather than leaving the decision of life or death either to their own Executive or to the unpredictable actions of one faction or another in a quarrel within a foreign country.

We urgently request that you call the Congress into immediate session.